Data Quality and
High-Dimensional
Data Analysis

Proceedings of the DASFAA 2008 Workshops

Data Quality and High-Dimensional Data Analysis

Proceedings of the DASFAA 2008 Workshops

Chee-Yong Chan
National University of Singapore, Singapore

Sanjay Chawla
University of Sydney, Australia

Shazia Sadiq
University of Queensland, Australia

Xiaofang Zhou
University of Queensland, Australia

Vikram Pudi
IIIT Hyderabad, India

World Scientific

NEW JERSEY · LONDON · SINGAPORE · BEIJING · SHANGHAI · HONG KONG · TAIPEI · CHENNAI

Published by

World Scientific Publishing Co. Pte. Ltd.

5 Toh Tuck Link, Singapore 596224

USA office: 27 Warren Street, Suite 401-402, Hackensack, NJ 07601

UK office: 57 Shelton Street, Covent Garden, London WC2H 9HE

British Library Cataloguing-in-Publication Data
A catalogue record for this book is available from the British Library.

ISBN-13 978-981-4273-48-0
ISBN-10 981-4273-48-1

Printed in Singapore.

PREFACE

The *First International Workshop on Data Quality in Collaborative Information Systems* was held in conjunction with the 13th International Conference on Database Systems for Advanced Applications, 19-22nd March, 2008, in New Delhi, India. The present volume contains the texts for four accepted papers and two invited papers presented at the workshop, as well as one additional paper presented at the co-located workshop on analysis of high dimensional discrete data.

Poor data quality is known to compromise the credibility and efficiency of commercial as well as public endeavours. Several developments from industry as well as academia have contributed significantly towards addressing the problem. These typically include analysts and practitioners who have contributed to the design of strategies and methodologies for data governance; solution architects including software vendors who have contributed towards appropriate system architectures that promote data integration and; and data experts who have contributed to data quality problems such as duplicate detection, identification of outliers, consistency checking and many more through the use of computational techniques. The attainment of true data quality lies at the convergence of the three aspects, namely organizational, architectural and computational.

At the same time, importance of managing data quality has increased manifold in today's global information sharing environments, as the diversity of sources, formats and volume of data grows. In this workshop we target data quality in the light of collaborative information systems where data creation and ownership is increasingly difficult to establish. Collaborative settings are evident in enterprise systems, where partner/customer data may pollute enterprise data bases raising the need for data source attribution, as well as in scientific applications, where data lineage across long running collaborative scientific processes needs to be established. Collaborative settings thus warrant a pipeline of data quality methods and techniques that commence with (source) data assessment, data cleansing, methods for sustained quality, integration and linkage, and eventually ability for audit and attribution.

The workshop was intended to provide a forum to bring together diverse researchers and make a consolidated contribution to new and extended methods to address the challenges of data quality in collaborative settings. Topics covered by the workshop include at least the following: Data linkage and fusion, Entity resolution, duplicate detection, and consistency checking, Data profiling and preparation, Use of data mining for data quality assessment, Methods for data transformation, reconciliation, consolidation, Data lineage and provenance, Models, frameworks, methodologies and metrics for data quality, Application specific data quality, case studies, and experience reports.

We would like to extend our appreciation and gratitude to the program committee of the workshop, who provided valuable reviews of submitted papers, and ensured the quality of the accepted papers and success of the workshop.

Nick Koudas, University of Toronto Markus Helfert, Dublin City University Floris Geerts, University of Edinburgh Xuemin Lin, University of New South Wales Rosanne Price, The University of Melbourne Wasim Sadiq, SAP Research Graeme Shanks, University of Melbourne Diane Strong, Worcester Polytechnic Institute Kerry Taylor, CSIRO ICT Centre Harry Zhu, Old Dominion University

We would also like to thank the keynote speaker of the workshop, *Prof. Divesh Srivastava*, from AT&T Labs-Research for his inspiring talk on "The Bellman data quality browser".

Last but not least, we would like to acknowledge the authors of the papers presented at the workshop, and thank them for their valuable contributions to the workshop as well as to the challenging and diverse area of data quality.

Shazia Sadiq, Xiaofang Zhou   The University of Queensland.
Organizing Co-chairs   April, 2008

ORGANIZING COMMITTEES

DASFAA Workshop Co-Chairs

Chee-Yong Chan   – National University of Singapore, Singapore
Sanjay Chawla   – University of Sydney, Australia

Publication Chair

Vikram Pudi   – IIIT Hyderabad, India

Workshop Organizers

Shazia Sadiq   – University of Queensland, Brisbane, Australia
Xiaofang Zhou   – University of Queensland, Brisbane, Australia

Program Committee

Nick Koudas   – University of Toronto
Markus Helfert   – Dublin City University
Floris Geerts   – University of Edinburgh
Xuemin Lin   – University of New South Wales
Rosanne Price   – The University of Melbourne
Wasim Sadiq   – SAP Research
Graeme Shanks   – University of Melbourne
Diane Strong   – Worcester Polytechnic Institute
Kerry Taylor   – CSIRO ICT Centre
Harry Zhu   – Old Dominion University

CONTENTS

Genomic Information Quality

Extended Abstract

Qing Liu

CSIRO Tasmanian ICT Centre, Australia
E-mail: Q.Liu@csiro.au

Xuemin Lin

The University of New South Wales, Australia
E-mail: lxue@cse.unsw.edu.au

1. Introduction

In the last 10 years we have witnessed the sequencing of the human genome and then the explosion in genomic data available in reference public databases and special purpose information products. These advances have profound influence in biology and drug discovery. Biological research has transformed from a purely experimental to an information-driven discovery science.

The quality of genomic information in the public and private database is crucial important. For example, to make a single drug useful, the pharmaceutical companies investigate how to generate proper structure of drug which is derived from experimental genomic data. The whole process of development, testing and clinical trials is extremely expensive. Using incorrect genomic information leads to the whole process failed. Further more, the cost is far more than merely financial. It also have great impact on trust from customers and motivation from workers etc.

In this paper, first, we will study the genomic information process and the errors produced during the process. Second, the key components of information quality theory will be reviewed. The genomic information quality problem is then presented.

2. Genomic Information Processing

The central dogma of molecular biology represents the genomic information process within an organism's cells (see Figure 1). Transcription is the process by which genetic information from DNA is transferred into RNA. During translation, the RNA sequence is translated into a sequence of amino acids as the protein, the building block of the body, is formed. Genomic data is about every piece of information involved in the above process. The data types involved include DNA sequence, gene expression, protein sequence, 3-dimensional protein, structural/functional annotation, metabolic/signalling pathway etc.

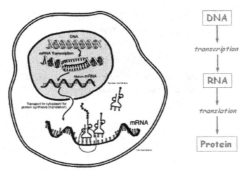

Fig. 1.   Central Dogma of Molecular Biology

To understand the information process for drug development and disease prevention, typical discovery process is that biological experiment is designed based on literature and experiments are performed on the living organism by wet-lab biologists. The result is transformed into digital data format using some platforms such as Affymetrix. Then data is analyzed by bioinformaticians using computer software. Biologists re-use the analyzed information to design more relevant and accurate experiment. From the above process, we can see the genomic information production is an inter-dependent process.

Various experiment and analysis steps may be involved based on the biological question studied. The overall process of genomic information production includes four dependent steps:

- Step 1: DNA sequence determination
- Step 2: genome feature annotation
- Step 3: protein sequence determination
- Step 4: protein function annotation

In each step, various errors caused by experiment, analysis etc. may occur. Muller and Naumann[1] provide a good classification of possible errors produced during the genomic information production.

- Experimental errors: unnoticed experimental setup failure or systematical errors
- Analysis errors: misinterpretation of information
- Transformation errors: information is not transferred properly from one representation into another
- Propagated errors: erroneous data is used for the generation of new data
- Stale data: unnoticed changes to base data on which a data item depends and that falsify it

Note analysis error is due to the misinterpretation of information. Incomplete or uncertain domain knowledge may lead to misinterpretation. The complexity of accessing heterogenous genomic data sources, in which the contents are overlapping or even conflicting, is also another major reason of misinterpretation.

Table 1 shows the summary of possible errors in each step. Interested readers may refer[1] for details.

Table 1. Possible Error Produced During Genomic Information Production

Step	Experimental error	Analysis error	Transformation error	Propagated error	Stale data
1	✓		✓		
2		✓		✓	✓
3	✓		✓	✓	✓
4	✓	✓		✓	✓

Information Quality Theory

Klein and Rossin mentioned there is no single definition of data quality accepted by researchers and those working in the discipline.[2] And "fitness for use"[3] is widely adopted in the quality literatures.

In the context of information quality assessment, three key components are presented by Ge and Helfert:[4] identification of quality problem, identification of quality dimension and assessment methodology.

Quality problem: There are three types of quality problems summarized by Garvin:[5] biased information, outdate information and massaged information.

- Biased information: the content of the information is inaccurate or distorted in the transformation process
- Outdate information: the information that is not up to date for the task
- Massaged information: the different representations of the same information

Quality dimension: It is also confirmed that quality is a multi-dimensional concept. Intuitive, theoretical and empirical methods are three approaches to study the quality.[6] By intuitive approach, quality dimension are based on the specific application contexts. Theoretical approach define quality dimension by data deficiencies. The data fitness for use to data consumers are the main quality dimension of empirical approach.

Assessment methodology: To assess the quality, Pipino et al. classify the assessment into objective and subjective assessment.[7] Objective assessment is to measure the extent to which information conforms to quality specifications and references. Subjective assessment is to measure the extent to which information is fitness for use by data consumers.

3. Genomic Information Quality

From the above two sections, a natural mapping could be found from the genomic information error produced during the genomic information generation to the information quality problems (see Table 2).

Table 2.   Mapping Between Information Quality Problem and Genomic Information Error

Quality Problem	Genomic Information Error
biased information	transformation error, propagated error, experimental error
outdated information	stale data
massaged information	analysis error

Some work has been done to improve the genomic information quality. Martinez and Hammer[8] extended an existing data model to include quality metadata. In,[9] a framework for the declarative specification of a user's personal quality processing requirement is proposed. Data integration approaches are also adopted in this domain.

Many research efforts have been put to apply quality theory to various application context, such as data warehousing, decision making, finance etc. However, very few work has been aimed at applying quality theory to genomic information quality even the problems studied are matched.

One of the fundamental problems with quality measurement in this domain is the lack of agreement on common quality dimension, and of practical instruments for performing quality assessments.

Some progresses have been made to set the foundation towards genomic data quality control standards for gene expression data.[10] However, much efforts are required to address whole genomic information quality.

4. Conclusion

Genomic information is dirty and errors could not be avoided due to the complex information production process. Building genomic data quality standards will substantially reduce analysis cost by reducing the need for replicate experiments and in turn, speed up the drug discovery and disease prevention. Another benefit is that genomic data quality standards will facilitate future technology development. When established standards exist, it is much easier to conduct proof-of-principle studies using new systems.[10]

References

1. H. Müller and F. Naumann, Data quality in genome databases, in *Information Quality*, eds. M. J. Eppler and M. Helfert (MIT, 2003).
2. B. D. Klein and D. F. Rossin, *Data Quality* **5** (1999).
3. F. G. Joseph M. Juran and R. Bingham, *Quality Control Handbook* (McGraw-Hill, New York, 1974).
4. M. Ge and M. Helfert, A review of information quality research - develop a research agenda, in *The International Conference of Information Quality*, (Cambridge, Massachusetts, USA, 2007).
5. D. A. Garvin, *Managing Quality* (Free Press, 1988).
6. R. Y. Wang and D. M. Strong, *Journal of Management Information System.* **12**, 5 (1996).
7. L. L. Pipino, Y. W. Lee and R. Y. Wang, *Commun. ACM* **45**, 211 (2002).
8. A. Martinez and J. Hammer, Making quality count in biological data sources, in *IQIS '05: Proceedings of the 2nd international workshop on Information quality in information systems*, (ACM, New York, NY, USA, 2005).
9. P. Missier, S. Embury, M. Greenwood, A. Preece and B. Jin, Quality views: capturing and exploiting the user perspective on data quality, in *VLDB '06: Proceedings of the 32nd international conference on Very large data bases*, (VLDB Endowment, 2006).
10. H. Ji and R. W. Davis, *Nature Biotechnology* **24**, 112 (2006).

DeepDetect: An Extensible System for Detecting Attribute Outliers & Duplicates in XML

Qiangfeng Peter Lau,   Wynne Hsu,   Judice L. Y. Koh,   and   Mong Li Lee

School of Computing
National University of Singapore
{plau, whsu, jkoh, leeml} @comp.nus.edu.sg

XML, the eXtensible Markup Language, is fast evolving into the new standard for data representation and exchange on the WWW. This has resulted in a growing number of data cleaning techniques to locate "dirty" data (artifacts). In this paper, we present DEEPDETECT – an extensible system that detects attribute outliers and duplicates in XML documents. Attribute outlier detection finds objects that contain deviating values with respect to a relevant group of objects. This entails utilizing the correlation among element values in a given XML document. Duplicate detection in XML requires the identification of subtrees that correspond to real world objects. Our system architecture enables sharing of common operations that prepare XML data for the various artifact detection techniques. DEEPDETECT also provides an intuitive visual interface for the user to specify various parameters for preprocessing and detection, as well as to view results.

Keywords: XML, data quality, data cleaning, duplicate detection, attribute outlier detection

1. Introduction

Data overload, combined with the widespread use of automated large-scale analysis and mining, has led to the rapid depreciation of data quality. Data cleaning is an emerging domain that aims at improving data quality through the detection and elimination of artifacts. We define artifacts to comprise of errors, discrepancies, redundancies, ambiguities, and incompleteness that hamper the efficacy of analysis or data mining. Recent years have seen a rapid proliferation of semi-structured data models such as XML (eXtensible Markup Language) as a new standard for data representation and exchange on the WWW. Increasingly more databases are converted into XML formats to facilitate data access and integration, for example, the UniProt database of the worldwide protein sequences.[1]

Despite the paradigm shift, development of data cleaning techniques for XML data is still at its infancy. Existing works mainly focus on duplicate detection in XML documents.[2-4] Outlier detection is also important in data cleaning, since outliers are often data noise or errors that diminish the accuracy of data mining. There are two types of outliers: class outliers and attribute outliers. A class outlier is a multivariate data point (tuple) which does not fit into any class by definitions of distance, density, or nearest-neighbor. An attribute outlier is a univariate point which exhibits deviating correlation behavior with respect to other attributes.[5] This work focuses on attribute outliers, and we use the term outlier interchangeably with attribute outlier.

XML data differs from relational data in several aspects that limit the direct adaptation of conventional detection methods. Moreover, the hierarchical relationships between the XML elements provide additional contextual information to the detection problem. This enables the separation of the XML document into smaller workable partitions.

In light of the need to be able to find artifacts in XML data, we design DEEPDETECT as an extensible system for detecting both attribute outliers and duplicates in XML documents. Outlier detection finds *objects* that contain deviating values (outliers) with respect to a relevant group of objects.[5,6] Duplicate detection in XML requires the identification of subtrees that corresponds to real-world objects for subsequent subtree matching.

In this paper, we describe the attribute outlier and duplicate detection capabilities of the DEEPDETECT system. DEEPDETECT is extensible – new artifact detection algorithms can be easily added based on our architecture. The system supports common preprocessing features and provides capabilities for the necessary correction of artifacts after detection. The graphical user interface of the system also makes it easy for novice users to configure and run the various artifact detection algorithms on XML documents.

2. Motivating Example

In this section, we use examples to illustrate the notions of attribute outliers and duplicates in XML documents.

2.1. *Attribute Outliers in XML*

We use the definitions in the XODDS framework[6] for the detection of attribute outliers in XML. We define an *object* as an instance of a related set of values that correspond to a real-world entity. For example, Fig. 1

shows an XML document containing bank accounts and their corresponding transactions. A *Transaction* object consists of the values of the elements: *Amt, Type,* and *Bank.* The leftmost *Transaction* object, denoted as
Obj(Transaction), is the set {⟨Amt/$30⟩, ⟨Type/C⟩, ⟨Bank/YZ⟩}.

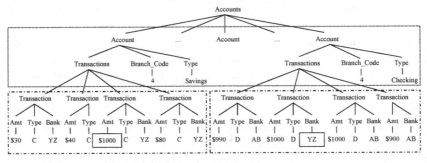

Fig. 1.   Example of Bank Account XML and Object Groupings (correlated subspaces)

The hierarchical structure of XML data serves to organize data according to their relevance – the closer the nearest shared ancestor is to the
two elements, the more relevant they are, where closeness is measured by
difference in ancestor-descendant element depth. In Fig. 1, the *Transactions* elements serve to organize relevant *Transaction* elements that are
made through the same *Account.* Likewise, the *Accounts* element serves
to organize the relevant *Account* elements. We refer to elements such as
Transactions and *Accounts* as *pivot* elements.

This notion of *pivot* elements allows partitioning of XML data into
groups of objects according to their relevance. Each partition can be analyzed for attribute outliers independently, aiding in the scalability of the
system. Furthermore, local outliers detected within a group of objects are
more meaningful than outliers detected across all objects. Figure 1 illustrates three such relevant groups (boxed), one for *Account* objects and two
for *Transaction* objects. When analyzing for transactional outliers, it is
more useful to detect them within the same bank account than across all
bank accounts. Hence transactions in the same bank account are grouped
together. Such related groupings are referred to as *correlated subspaces* that
are identifiable through the pivot elements.

An attribute outlier is a value in an object (the text of an XML element) that rarely occurs together with the other values in the same object
within a particular correlated subspace. For example, the solid-boxed values ⟨Amt/$1000⟩ and ⟨Bank/YX⟩ in Fig. 1 are outliers. ⟨Amt/$1000⟩, is an

outlier because it is an unusually high transaction amount with respect to the values for *Type* and *Bank* compared to other transactions in the same account. ⟨Bank/YX⟩ is an outlier as the other transactions with the similar values for *Type* and *Amt* all involve ⟨Bank/AB⟩ instead. A subset of the elements for each transaction object is used to compute for outlier-ness and is referred to as the *correlated neighbors*.

Measuring outlier-ness involves counting the *supports* of correlated neighbors within correlated subspaces and comparing them. For example, the support of the correlated neighbor, {⟨Type/C⟩, ⟨Bank/YZ⟩}, of the correlated subspace given by the left *Transactions* element in Fig. 1, is 3 since it appears thrice in the subspace. Two measures of outlier-ness were given in,[6] namely the *xO-measure* and *xQ-measure* that measures outliers within correlated subspaces, whereby a smaller value indicates a higher degree of outlier-ness.

It is interesting to note that the outliers do not necessarily indicate error in data; they can be the result of suspicious activity that may have legal implications, as in the case of our Bank Account example. Hence, this is an added benefit of the ability to detect attribute outliers in a cleaning system.

2.2. *Duplicates in XML*

A real-world object (e.g. a movie, a CD, etc) can be mapped to a set of elements in an XML document. We call this set of elements an entity[a]. Duplicate detection aims to find clusters of duplicate *entities* in the XML document.

For example, in Fig. 1, if the intention is to detect duplicate transactions across all bank accounts, then we can map a transaction in the real world to the entity that comprises of the three XML elements: *Amt*, *Type*, and *Bank*. However, if the intent is to detect duplicate transactions within the same bank account, then the entity should include an additional XML element such as the unique account information, *Account_ID* (not shown in Fig. 1), to discriminate against transactions in other accounts. Hence, depending on the application, a domain expert is needed to identify the entity in the XML documents.

Having identified the entities, similarities between entities are computed as follows. We first use edit distance to determine the similarity between the values of each corresponding pair of elements in the entity. Two elements are similar if their edit distance is below some user-defined threshold. Next,

---

[a]Note that an entity, like an object, is an embodiment of a real-world object.

we apply a weighted sum of the element pair similarities to compute the overall similarity between a pair of entities. If the overall similarity is below some threshold, then we can conclude that they are likely to refer to the same real-world object.

3. Architecture

In this section, we describe the main components of the DEEPDETECT system. As shown in Fig. 2, DEEPDETECT comprises of a GUI module, a Specification module, a Data Preparation module and an Artifact Detection module.

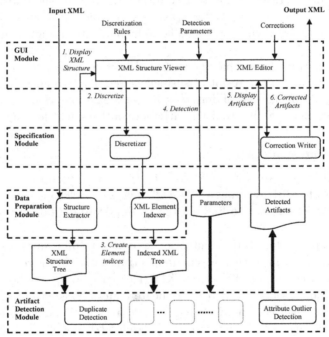

Fig. 2.   DEEPDETECT System Architecture

3.1. *GUI Module*

This module consists of two main viewer components, the *XML Structure Viewer* and the *XML Editor*. The *XML Structure Viewer* is a tree-like viewer that allows the users to explore the XML structure. The viewer also collects user specification for discretization and input parameters required for the various artifact detection tasks. The *XML Editor* displays the detected artifacts' locations and allows the user to specify corrections (if necessary). Furthermore, it also displays the abbreviated XPaths of the XML elements related to the artifacts so that the user may use external applications to query specific portions of the XML document.

3.2. *Specification Module*

This module encompasses the input and output specification for the data cleaning process. The *Discretizer* groups the input numerical values according to the discretization interval width as specified by the user. The transformed XML data is used as input to the various artifact detection processes. The *Correction Writer* is responsible for exporting the output XML document with user corrections that were previously specified through the XML editor interface.

3.3. *Data Preparation Module*

The data preparation module converts the XML document to an internal representation that facilitates the detection of artifacts. The *Structure Extracter* automatically processes the XML document to build a structure tree and determine the multiplicity of the elements. This can be achieved through a depth-first traversal of the XML tree. A node is created for each unique element name. Each node has a hash table that provides fast access to elements with the same name. The result is a compact structure tree that describes the nesting of XML elements as shown in Fig. 3. In the process, "one" or "many" multiplicity of the XML elements are also identified.

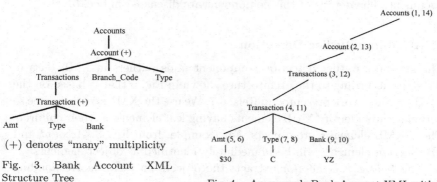

(+) denotes "many" multiplicity

Fig. 3. Bank Account XML Structure Tree

Fig. 4. An example Bank Account XML with traversal interval pair labels

The *XML Element Indexer* uses the interval-based labeling scheme to convert the XML document to an internal indexed representation for faster lookup during processing. XML elements are divided into different files based on the element names. A depth-first traversal is performed on the XML tree starting from the root. In each XML element's index, the *start* and *end* order of traversal is recorded as a traversal interval pair (s, e). For example, in Fig. 4, starting from the root element, *Accounts*, the *Transaction* element will have the interval (4, 11), while its children, $\langle Amt/\$30\rangle$, $\langle Type/C\rangle$, and $\langle Bank/YZ\rangle$ will have the intervals (5, 6), (7, 8), and (9, 10) respectively. Note that the intervals for the descendant nodes are always bounded by the ancestors' intervals. In addition, during indexing, the element depth and the abbreviated XPath is also determined and stored. With this, we can maintain the order of appearance of the XML elements in the original XML document.

3.4. *Artifact Detection Module*

This module contain the key components for detecting the various artifacts. The architecture is extensible with additional detection routines which may make use of the same specification and data preparation capabilities.

The *Attribute Outlier Detection* component projects correlated subspaces and does support counting before applying a user specified metric to evaluate outliers. The details of this component is discussed in Sec. 4.

The *Duplicate Detection* component extracts the duplicate candidates from user specified entities. Candidate entities are compared to identify duplicate clusters. The result of this process is a list of detected duplicate clusters that the user may choose to eliminate from the output XML document. The details of this component are discussed in Sec. 5.

4. Attribute Outlier Detection

The attribute outlier detection component finds outliers in XML data in the steps according to the architecture shown in Fig. 5 that is based on the XODDS framework presented in Refs. 6,7. We use the XML structure tree to automatically identify XML elements having leaf elements as their children. These XML elements are objects. For example, from Fig. 3, *Account* and *Transaction* elements will be immediately identified as object elements.

The *Subspace Generator* extracts the objects into their corresponding correlated subspaces. To do so, pivot elements must be identified. Given the XML structure tree, for a particular object, we can identify the name of the element that serves as the pivot element as follows:

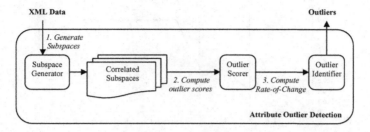

Fig. 5.   Outlier Detection Architecture

(1) Use the XML structure tree to find a path, P, from an object element v to the root element r.

(2) Suppose we have the path $P = v_0, ..., v_n$ where $v_0 = v$ is the object element and $v_n = r$ is the root element. Then the pivot element of the correlated subspace for v is the first occurrence of v_p, $1 \leq p \leq n$, s.t. v_{p-1} has an element multiplicity of "many".

Using the method above, in Fig. 3, we can identify *Transactions* as the pivot of *Transaction* and *Accounts* as the pivot of *Account*. Once the pivot elements are identified, grouping objects into correlated subspaces is a matter of placing all the elements that are descendants of the pivot element into the same subspace.

Once the correlated subspaces are generated, for each subspace, projections are made over the objects to generate their correlated neighbors. For example, the leftmost transaction object, $\{\langle Amt/<100\rangle, \langle Type/C\rangle, \langle Bank/YZ\rangle\}$ in Fig. 1 will have 7 correlated neighbors, namely:

- $\{\langle Amt/<100\rangle\}$,
- $\{\langle Type/C\rangle\}$,
- $\{\langle Bank/YZ\rangle\}$,
- $\{\langle Amt/<100\rangle, \langle Type/C\rangle\}$,
- $\{\langle Amt/<100\rangle, \langle Bank/YZ\rangle\}$,
- $\{\langle Type/C\rangle, \langle Bank/YZ\rangle\}$,
- $\{\langle Amt/<100\rangle, \langle Type/C\rangle, \langle Bank/YZ\rangle\}$.

The support of each neighbor is counted in the process.

From the support values, the *Outlier Scorer* computes the degree of outlier-ness, using the measures given in Ref. 6, as a *score*. Values that occur frequently are less likely to be outliers. Thus, to reduce score computation, these values are filtered when their counts are greater than a user specified *min_sup* threshold.

After the score for each potential outlier is calculated, the *Outlier Identifier* sorts them and an outlier threshold is automatically determined by computing the largest *rate-of-change* (difference between two adjacent scores). Note that there are cases where, due to the natural occurrences in

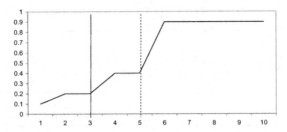

Fig. 6.   Plot of potential Outlier index versus score. A situation whereby rate-of-change admits too many false positives

the XML document, the *min_sup* threshold parameter used in the scorer fails to remove enough false positives. A hypothetical situation is shown in Fig. 6 that plots the potential outliers versus score. Computing the rate-of-change will give a cut-off threshold at the 5th potential outlier (dotted line) that might admit too many false positives. Such situations can be remedied by introducing a "soft_cut" parameter, $k \in (0, 1]$, that only considers the the top $k \times n$ out of n potential outliers when computing the rate of change. For example, setting $k = 0.5$ for the situation in Fig. 6 will first discard the 6th to 10th potential outliers. Then, the resulting rate-of-change will give a cut-off threshold at the 3rd potential outlier.

Potential outliers with scores below the cut-off threshold are marked as outliers. Finally, objects that contain these outliers are returned to the front-end of the system to be highlighted to the user.

5. Duplicate Detection

The duplicate detection component is shown in Fig. 7. An *entity definition* is a mapping of a real-world object to a set of XML element names as well as a set of thresholds, Θ. A *tuple* is a pair of element name and its corresponding value. An *entity* consists of a set of tuples that conforms to an entity definition. For example, in Fig. 1, using the definition of a transaction entity given in Fig. 8, the leftmost transaction entity comprises of the set of tuples {⟨Amt,$30⟩, ⟨Type,C⟩, ⟨Bank,YZ⟩}.

The duplicate detection process begins with the XML data and entity definitions as input. The *Extractor* module extracts entities in the XML documents that correspond to the entity definitions. These are the duplicate candidates. In the process, the Extractor also generates the unique tuples from the candidate entities. Note that the duplicate candidates are extracted from the internally indexed XML document instead of the original document. This allows more direct access to the XML data through the

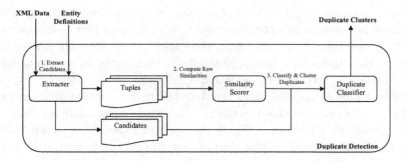

Fig. 7.   Duplicate Detection Architecture

indices created by the XML Element Indexer.

The *Similarity Scorer* computes the pair-wise similarity between the text strings in tuples belonging to the same XML element based on their edit distance (Levenshtein) normalized to the length of the longer string. Each $\theta \in \Theta$ specified in the entity definition that corresponds to an XML element is used as a threshold to filter dissimilar pairs of tuples.

The *Duplicate Classifier* uses the tuples of candidate entities to build a directed graph.[8] This facilitates the direct access of the tuples of an entity. Figure 9 illustrates an example sub-graph of two entities from the graph used for computing duplicate entities. Vertices t_1 and t_2 refer to the first and third leftmost Transaction entities from Fig. 1. Note that vertices representing tuples ⟨Type, C⟩ and ⟨Bank, YZ⟩ are connected to both t_1 and t_2 since these entities share the exact same unique tuples.

Element	Threshold
Amt	0.5
Type	0.5
Bank	0.4

Fig. 8.   Example Entity Definition for Bank Transactions

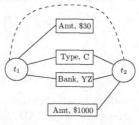

Note that a line with no arrowheads indicate bi-directional edge. The dotted line denotes a special edge connecting duplicate entities

Fig. 9.   Example sub-graph of two Transaction entities

If two tuples are similar (as scored previously), directed edges are added from one tuple vertex to the entity vertices adjacent to the other tuple vertex. For example, in Fig. 9, if tuples ⟨Amt, $30⟩ and ⟨Amt, $1000⟩ are scored as being similar, the edges $(\langle \text{Amt}, \$30 \rangle, t_2)$ and $(\langle \text{Amt } \$1000 \rangle, t_1)$ will be added. In this way, an entity's similarity with another may be computed based on the number of paths from the entity vertex, through one tuple vertex to the other entity vertex. Examples of such paths from t_1 to t_2 are: $t_1 \to \langle \text{Type, C} \rangle \to t_2$, and $t_1 \to \langle \text{Bank, YZ} \rangle \to t_2$.

Once a pair of entities, u, v, are detected to be duplicates, a special duplicate edge (u, v) is added to the graph. For example, assuming that t_1 and t_2 qualify as duplicates in Fig. 9, the dotted line represents a duplicate edge. Computing the transitive closure over the subgraph formed by vertices linked by duplicate edges gives the duplicate clusters. These duplicate clusters are returned to the front-end of the system to be highlighted to the user.

6. Implementation

DEEPDETECT is implemented in JAVA. In order to handle large XML documents, DEEPDETECT is implemented using the Xerces SAX XML parser[9] instead of the DOM parser as the DOM tree consumes too much main memory. The SAX parser returns a series of events (e.g. encountering the start tag of an element) when parsing to a event handler instead of returning a data-structure. We use an event chaining mechanism in which one event handler passes event information to another handler so that multiple operations can be handled in a single parse of the XML document. This is shown schematically in Fig. 10. Note that a handler may fork the events to two separate handlers as in the case of Handler 1.

Fig. 10.   Example event handler chaining

When loading a new XML document, DEEPDETECT is able to discern an XML's structure. The XML file is copied to a separate storage directory to ensure subsequent modifications to it will not affect the original data. The copy step is done through the parser, thus allowing validation of the XML file. This is an example where copying and discerning the XML's structure can be done in a single pass using event handler chaining.

One common operation when detecting artifacts is counting the occurrences of data. Although hash tables are commonly used to do so, for large XML documents, unique data may require hash tables that are too big to fit in main memory. In such cases, a combination of size bounded hash tables and multi-pass approaches over the XML data is used.

For the implementation of the Outlier Detection component, there is the possibility of combinatorial explosion for high arity objects when data is sparse in relation to the size of the XML document. Hence projections on subspaces are done incrementally with intermediate results written to disk at the expense of computation time. To reduce the space consumed on disk, standard text compression is used.

7. Features

Figure 11 displays the preprocessing screen of DeepDetect on a sample XML document of a Compact Disc (CD) catalog. The user is presented with the XML tree structure. We provide a point and click interface for the user to specify the exact position in the tree structure to apply discretization rules in this preprocessing step. The values of elements that correspond to the specified element names will be discretized. For example, Fig. 11 shows that the PRICE elements will be discretized using the bin width of 1.

To begin detecting artifacts, we provide the user with a unified configuration screen to choose which artifact detection algorithms to employ as shown in Fig. 12.

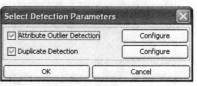

Fig. 12.   Choosing which detection algorithms to include

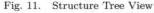

Fig. 11.   Structure Tree View

Fig. 13.   Making corrections

Attribute outlier detection is primarily conducted by a number of back-end processes with minimal user interaction. The user specifies the required parameters such as *min_sup* and the soft-cut through the unified configuration screen.

Duplicate detection requires users to specify the entity definitions in detail. Hence we provide automatic creation of entity definitions by choosing entities based on elements with leaf elements as children. These entity definitions may then be customized (or removed) to suit the user's requirements. Figure 14 shows editing an example definition of a CD entity that contains all its children elements.

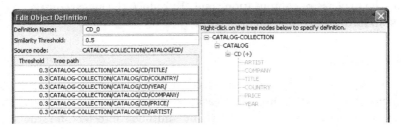

Fig. 14.　Customizing entity definition for duplicate detection

Once the required parameters for the chosen artifact detection algorithms have been entered, the system discretizes and builds an internal indexed representation of the XML document. This is followed by applying the various detection processes to identify outliers and duplicates.

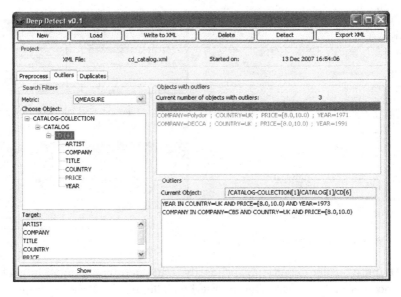

Fig. 15.　Viewing identified objects that contain outliers

After detection, objects identified to contain attribute outliers may be browsed by the user. For each such object, the outliers are displayed together with the projection on the object that they are detected in. Figure 15 shows some highlighted CD objects with outliers. In particular the current CD object has ⟨YEAR/1973⟩ as an outlier in {⟨COUNTRY/UK⟩, ⟨PRICE/[8,10)⟩, ⟨YEAR/1973⟩} which may indicate that most CDs in the data set are not priced at the range between [8, 10) in the UK during 1973. The unique XML element keys for each object, similar to XPath, is also displayed for identification.

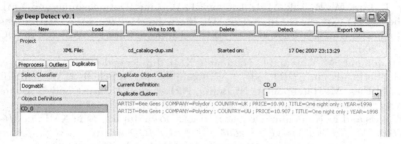

Fig. 16.   Viewing duplicate clusters

Next, the duplicate clusters identified are also highlighted to the user. Figure 16 illustrates two duplicate CD entities. Note that they both have exactly the same tuples for ⟨ARTIST, Bee Gees⟩ and ⟨TITLE, One night⟩ only. Furthermore, their tuples for elements COMPANY, PRICE, COUNTRY, and YEAR are highly similar.

The detected artifacts and their related XML elements and abbreviated XPaths are shown to the user through the Correction Writer (see Fig. 13). Corrections made are saved and written when the XML file is exported. Alternatively the user may use the XPath information provided with other XML querying systems to make corrections.

8. Conclusion

In conclusion, we have presented the architecture of an extensible system, DEEPDETECT, that provides common components for detecting the various forms of artifacts or dirty data in XML documents. These common components provide preprocessing, indexing of XML data and correction capabilities. An overview of how attribute outliers in XML data are identified based on the XODDS framework is given. We also described how duplicates are detected. The detected artifacts are mapped to the XML elements in the original XML document for identification. We provided a brief insight into the handling of large XML documents. Our graphical interface facilitates the specifications for preprocessing, artifact detection, viewing of detected artifacts, and data correction by a novice user.

References

1. R. Apweiler, A. Bairoch, C. Wu, W. Barker, B. Boeckmann, S. Ferro, E. Gasteiger, H. Huang, R. Lopez and M. M. et al., *Nucleic Acids Res.* **32**, D115 (2004).
2. W. L. Low, W. H. Tok, M. L. Lee and T. W. Ling, Data cleaning and XML: The DBLP experience, in *ICDE '02: Proceedings of the 18th International Conference on Data Engineering*, (IEEE Computer Society, Washington, DC, USA, 2002).
3. S. Puhlmann, M. Weis and F. Naumann, XML duplicate detection using sorted neighborhoods., in *EDBT*, eds. Y. E. Ioannidis, M. H. Scholl, J. W. Schmidt, F. Matthes, M. Hatzopoulos, K. Böhm, A. Kemper, T. Grust and C. Böhm, Lecture Notes in Computer Science, Vol. 3896 (Springer, 2006).
4. M. Weis and F. Naumann, Dogmatix tracks down duplicates in XML, in *SIGMOD '05: Proceedings of the 2005 ACM SIGMOD international conference on Management of data*, (ACM Press, New York, NY, USA, 2005).
5. J. Koh, M. Lee, W. Hsu and K. Lam, Correlation-based detection of attribute outliers, in *12th International Conference on Database Systems for Advanced Applications*, (Bangkok, Thailand, 2007).
6. J. Koh, M. Lee, W. Hsu and W. T. Ang, Correlation-based attribute outlier detection in XML, in *Proceedings of the 24th International Conference on Data Engineering*, (Cancun, Mexico, 2008).
7. J. Koh, M. Lee, W. Hsu and W. T. Ang, *Correlation-based Attribute Outlier Detection in XML*, Tech. Rep. TRB6/07, National University of Singapore (2007).
8. M. Weis and F. Naumann, Detecting duplicate objects in xml documents, in *IQIS '04: Proceedings of the 2004 international workshop on Information quality in information systems*, (ACM, New York, NY, USA, 2004).
9. http://xerces.apache.org/, Xerces Simple API for XML Parser.

CHARIOT: A Comprehensive Data Integration and Quality Assurance Model for Agro-Meteorological Data

Mark Anthony F. Mateo   and   Carson Kai-Sang Leung*

Department of Computer Science, The University of Manitoba,
Winnipeg, MB, Canada   R3T 2N2
* E-mail: kleung@cs.umanitoba.ca
www.cs.umanitoba.ca/~kleung

In this paper, we propose a comprehensive data integration and quality assurance model, called CHARIOT, for agro-meteorological data. This model comprised of two modules: an *intermediary* module and a *data quality control* module. The intermediary provides users with reliable and continuous access to heterogeneous weather databases from various sources; it also solves various compatibility issues in meteorological time series data. The data quality control tool consists of a multi-layer system spanning internal, temporal and spatial data checks. These two modules combined together provide users with clean and error-free inputs for weather-driven agricultural management decisions. When applying CHARIOT to weather data for a real-life agricultural application, CHARIOT is shown to be effective in controlling and improving data quality, which in turn leads to better and more accurate agricultural management decisions.

Keywords: Data quality; Application; Weather observations; Consistency checking; Outlier detection.

1. Introduction

Agricultural yield and production are closely tied to the weather observed in a geographical area. Farmers base their crop management decisions on weather forecasts. Having accurate weather information helps farmers to make wise management decisions on their farms. This is especially important in the Prairie Provinces of Canada as well as in countries such as India, where agriculture forms a sizeable part of the economy.

Over the years, various agricultural decision support tools have used weather parameters as their inputs. For example, potato disease severity value tools,[1] which are used by farmers as a guide when to administer fungicides to combat the potato late blight disease, rely on temperature and relative humidity as inputs. As another example, neural network temperature predictors for frost[2] rely on historical weather observations. Both examples depend on historical and current weather observations. Any unusual observation may render inaccurate forecasts to the farmers.

Moreover, different national weather bureaux have continuously gathered weather observation data for their own historical records. These data have been stored in a format that is usually *prescribed* and *deemed appropriate during that time*. For instance, during the early years of computing, weather data were stored in flat file format in file systems. In the 1980s, the data were stored in relational database systems. With advances in technology, several organizations—such as the US National Weather Service (www.weather.gov/xml)—have recently stored their data in the XML format. Since different formats exist for different databases, there is a need to integrate them into a universally-intelligible format so as to make different datasets compatible for collaborative use. One solution is to re-implement older databases so that they would be adaptable to work with newer systems. However, this solution is *not* always practical. First, it is expensive in cost, manpower and time due to the sheer size of weather databases. To elaborate, as collaborative data sharing and usage among heterogeneous databases were not prevalent in the past, older systems were designed and implemented where inter-platform data exchanges were not seriously considered. Databases varied from country to country with no unique global standards to follow. This entailed not only understanding each national data format but also understanding the scripts used to display the data. Second, there is a need to keep databases functioning all the time. Adapting old systems to work with newer ones can have these systems pulled out of service for a significant amount of time that many applications cannot afford. Third, most of the old systems still respond to the current data, keeping the needs of their respective organizations. Having a new database may not be seen as practical because it will necessitate additional training for database administrators, which could be expensive and time consuming.

With advances in database technology, large amounts of weather data have been generated from various sources and gathered manually or automatically. For example, during the early days, a staff member manually recorded an observed reading from a meter and brought the recorded data to his headquarters for further data analysis. At present, data from wired and wireless weather stations are usually transmitted automatically via an electronic link to a centralized database for storage. In both instances, data might be subjected to collection and transmission errors, resulting in the data being inaccurate or corrupted. Manual observations are prone to human error and measurement subjectivity. Wireless networks are sometimes congested, where interferences and spikes are not uncommon, resulting in data being lost or inaccurately received during transmission. All of these scenarios can result in incorrect data observations, which may then be fed into some agricultural decision support tools resulting in wrong, anomalous or misleading forecasts. To a further extent, useless or misleading forecasts may in turn affect decisions made on which these tools were designed for (*e.g.*, crop management decision such as fungicide application). Hence, for successful and more accurate outputs from these agricultural decision support tools, it is vital for inputs to be clean[3-6] and to meet data quality requirements (*e.g.*, accuracy, completeness, timeliness and consistency).[6-9]

In the province of Manitoba in Canada, the provincial government department responsible for agriculture—Manitoba Agriculture, Food and Rural Initiatives (MAFRI)—operates a real-time weather monitoring network that collects agro-meteorological data. These data, together with archival observations from the Canadian national weather bureau—Environment Canada (www.ec.gc.ca)—as well as nearby weather stations in the US, are used by MAFRI in its agricultural decision support tools to help farmers make crop management decisions. With these data, we have the following questions: How can we process non-compatible data from heterogeneous databases? How can we make the data from different weather databases to have a uniform data format without re-implementing the databases or interrupting their operation? How can we assure that the weather data are clean? How can we identify unclean, incorrect or suspicious data?

In this paper, we answer these questions. We propose and develop a comprehensive data integration and quality assurance model for agrometeorological data (CHARIOT). Our *key contributions of this paper* include the following:

- the proposal of a data *intermediary* that encompasses and integrates heterogeneous databases of various eras, data formats and national standards—without re-implementing individual databases; and

- the development of a comprehensive multi-layer *quality control tool* that detects and identifies suspicious data so that these data can be further analyzed and verified whether they are *truly exceptional* or *invalid*.

It is important to note that CHARIOT integrates heterogeneous weather databases to present a *standardized view* for weather data inter-usage. This is essential for agricultural decision support tools to be able to rely on historical weather observations because they may use older non-compatible database platforms, which unavoidably are the key sources of archival weather data. With this, more accurate agricultural decision support tools will be available as their data inputs are clean, consistent and error-free.

This paper is organized as follow. The next section gives related work and background. Then, we start describing our proposed CHARIOT model, which consists of two modules. Specifically, we present the *data quality control module* and the *data intermediary module* in Sections 3 and 4 respectively. Section 5 shows experimental results on real-life agro-meteorological data. The generalizability and future extension of our model are discussed in Section 6. Finally, Section 7 gives conclusions.

2. Related Work and Background

Many existing agricultural decision support tools are mostly dependant on the collected agro-meteorological observations. Agricultural yield and production are highly correlated to the agro-meteorological data observed (*e.g.*, relative humidity, precipitation levels, air temperature) in a certain geographical area. Useful knowledge discovered from these observations allows farmers to make successful management decisions in their farms. Nonetheless, having accurate agro-meteorological data gathering capability is essential to knowledge discovery from weather databases. In other words, to help farmers make wise decisions (which in turn help improve their yield and production and make them more competitive), one needs to have techniques that demonstrate and ensure the high quality of the collected data—the agro-meteorological observations. Unfortunately, many organizations do not use an automated approach for the assurance of data quality. Instead, staffs are often asked to visit each site or station regularly and fix problems (*e.g.*, malfunctioned measuring instruments) if they spot one. Once data are collected, staffs analyze the data manually using primitive methods. In general, such a manual approach is tedious and may simply lead to inaccurate results. Moreover, one may not be able to detect problems easily. This calls for better data quality control,[7–15] which (i) ensures that data meet quality requirements (*e.g.*, accuracy, completeness, timeliness, consistency) and (ii) flags any measurements that need further investigation. With better data quality control, we can feed more accurate data into our agricultural decision support tools so that better results or prediction can be achieved.

Over the past decade, various methods[16–18] have been proposed to detect erroneous meteorological observations. However, they suffer from some problems or lack some functionality. As a preview, we will compare some of these methods with our proposed CHARIOT model in Section 5.

Recently, we also dealt with agro-meteorological data. In one of our previous papers,[19] we proposed an intelligent computational model for agro-meteorological data. Specifically, we focused on constructing a neural network for trend prediction. In contrast, our current paper focuses on data integration and data quality assurance.

In another paper[20] of ours, we focused on the proposal of a generic model for controlling the quality of data. Techniques described in such a proposal can be applied to the development of a specific data quality control module for handling agro-meteorological data. However, our previous paper did not consider how to integrate data in different formats collected from various heterogeneous sources. Note that data integration is an important technical focus area of the current paper.

Regarding the data we used in this study, they were obtained from MAFRI. In the province of Manitoba in Canada, MAFRI administers the Manitoba Ag-Weather program—which aims to make farmers more competitive via weather-driven tools that provide agricultural decision support. These decision support tools (*e.g.*, those for potato and tomato disease forecasts) use both current and historical weather data (*e.g.*, temperature). In addition, data quality control—particularly for checking temporal consistency—is dependant on weather observations spanning the past few decades covering dense temporal data resolution and vast geographical jurisdictions. However, because historical data were stored in a way regarded as the most appropriate during that period, most of the old archival data are housed in legacy flat file systems—which are incompatible with current systems. As an example, Environment Canada maintains the Canadian National Climate Data and Information Archive, which is a well-maintained archive containing Canadian weather data as far back as the 1840s. This archive uses the legacy *flat file format*.

Besides the lack of functionality of existing methods and the varieties of data formats, changes in national measurement standards over the years can also cause problems in integrating data from heterogeneous sources. For example, Canada adopted metric units for measurement in the 1970s–1980s. All weather measurements prior to that time were made in Imperial units. To make pre-metric archival data usable in today's metric based agro-meteorological models, we need to find a way to efficiently convert a huge amount of weather observations spanning several decades. This scenario is not only confined with historical data but also with current ones. As in many other Canadian provinces, a vast majority of arable land in the province of

Manitoba is bordered by the US. To ensure greater geographical coverage and more accurate forecasts and models, Manitoban towns near the US border need to have collaborative data sharing from adjacent stations in the US state of North Dakota. However, the US still uses Imperial units, necessitating conversion procedures each time when US weather data are used.

3. Our Data Quality Control Module

In this project, our ultimate goal is to build a comprehensive data integration and quality assurance model suitable for agro-meteorological purposes. To achieve this goal, we develop the two key modules of this model: (i) the *data quality control module* and (ii) the *data intermediary module*. The resulting CHARIOT model serves multiple purposes. First, it identifies any data that appear to be incorrect or inconsistent. Second, it assures that data are both temporally and spatially consistent with their temporal and spatial neighbours. Third, it serves as an intermediary between heterogeneous agro-meteorological databases that uses different national standards and incompatible data representation formats deployed in different locations and time periods by solving problems such as incompatible data representation due to different database platforms, missing data and measurement unit incompatibilities (*e.g.*, Imperial vs. metric). While we describe our multi-layer data quality control module in this section, we will describe our intermediary module in Section 4.

3.1. *The internal layer for identifying incorrect data and inconsistent data*

As with any existing model, it is an established concept that "garbage in, garbage out". As a result, we need to ensure that data fed into the agricultural decision support tools are clean, or at least free of gross errors caused by data reporting inaccuracy, typographical errors, instrumental malfunction and measurement unit inconsistency. We also need to verify that the data fall within a valid range as defined by the climatologic records of the area. To clean and pre-process the data, we perform the following tasks at each of the more than 30 distributed stations scattered throughout the province of Manitoba:

(i) We identify errors such as (a) the daily maximum temperature at location *loc* on date *d* (denoted as $x_{maxTemp,\,d,\,loc}$) being cooler than its daily minimum temperature at the *same* location on the *same* date (denoted as $x_{minTemp, d, loc}$) and (b) the daily average temperature (denoted as $x_{avgTemp, d, loc}$) being warmer than the daily maximum temperature. Here, we guard our data quality module against "absurd" values for the weather parameters. Let us consider one weather parameter (say, temperature). We ensure that $x_{minTemp, d, loc} \leq x_{avgTemp, d, loc} \leq x_{maxTemp, d, loc}$ (*i.e.*, the daily minimum temperature does not exceed the daily average temperature, which in turn does not exceed the daily maximum temperature). Besides temperature, similar verification can be applied to other weather parameters such as relative humidity.

(ii) We compare the observed agro-meteorological data against extreme values based on archival climatologic records for the monthly high and low measurements in the specific area. If any of the following condition occurs, an observation is flagged for further investigation:

   (a) An observed (minimum, average or maximum) temperature value falls outside the record range of $[-60°C, +60°C]$;
   (b) An observed relative humidity value falls outside of the record range of $[0\%, 100\%]$;
   (c) An observed rainfall value falls outside of the record range of $[0mm, 190mm]$;
   (d) An observed value exceeds the maximum readings of the previous or the next months; or
   (e) An observed value falls below the minimum readings of the previous or the next months.

Note that it is unusual, but not impossible, to have a flagged observation (say, record-breaking temperature).

(iii) We identify errors with extraordinarily large daily range between minimum and maximum observed readings while these maximum and minimum measurements are within their reasonable ranges. For example, it may sound suspicious to have $x_{maxTemp, d, loc} - x_{minTemp, d, loc} \geq 24°C$ (where both $x_{maxTemp, d, loc}$ and $x_{minTemp, d, loc}$ lie within the record range of $[-60°C, +60°C]$) because it would be a very unusual weather phenomenon in Manitoba to have such a drastic change in temperature within a day. Hence, such a suspicious observation (if any) requires further investigation.

(iv) We also examine the observed values for serial continuity. Specifically, we check whether observations remain constant for some (say, at least three) consecutive days. Note that it is quite unusual, and may sound suspicious, to have long period of days with the *same* maximum or minimum temperature. Of course, there are some exceptions to this check. For example, while we flag a sequence of three or more consecutive *non-zero* rainfall measurements, we do not flag sequences of three or more consecutive *zero* precipitation measurements. While it is possible (and not uncommon) to have a long period of dry days, it sounds suspicious (though not impossible) to observe long period of rainy days with identical daily precipitation measurements (*e.g.*, daily rainfall of 100 mm for 10 consecutive days).

(v) We check our dataset for the presence of abrupt increase or decrease that remarkably deviates from the existing trend in the dataset. A short-lived data "spike" can be caused by either an equipment breakdown (then the "spike" is an anomalous observation) or a legitimate record-breaking observation. Here, we use some data mining algorithm (*e.g.*, a distance-based outlier detection algorithm[21]). We flag a data value $x_{attr,\ d,\ loc} \in DB$ as a "spike" if most data values in the dataset DB lie far away from $x_{attr,\ d,\ loc}$. For our particular application, we flag data having a "distance" of 5°C to 10°C as *suspicious data* (which is worthy of further investigation), and we mark for *automatic deletion* those observations having a "distance" > 10°C.

3.2. *The temporal layer for assuring the consistency of data with their sequential cycles*

Once the observed data have been cleaned and pre-processed of gross errors and inconsistencies, we check for their behaviour with respect to their temporal neighbours. Specifically, let us show—in this section—how the temporal layer of our CHARIOT model ensures that agro-meteorological data follow, or are consistent with, some sequential cycles.

In this layer, we compare the current observation with the historical one to evaluate if the current one is behaving consistently with the cycles established by the historical observations. Data observed on some date d in the current cycle are supposed to be consistent with data observed on d in previous and subsequent cycles.

To identify inconsistent data, the temporal layer first extracts relevant data from the time series. Without loss of generality, let us assume that data are collected on a daily basis and follow a yearly cycle. For each datum obtained on a certain date d (say, March 21, 2008), the temporal layer considers (i) datum for March 20, 2008, (ii) datum for March 22, 2008, and (iii) data for these three dates (March 20–22) in all previous and subsequent years. Note that this data extraction technique can be applicable for other cycles (*e.g.*, daily, weekly, monthly, quarterly or seasonal cycles).

To learn from historical data, we assume that a complete time-series archive of data is available. If this assumption does not hold, our data intermediary module (Section 4) takes over and provides strategies to solve various scenarios to ensure data completeness.

Once the temporal layer extracts relevant data from the time series and analyzes them, it computes the mean and standard deviation (specifically, the bi-weight mean $\overline{x}_{bw}$ and bi-weight standard deviation σ_{bw} measures[22]) of the time series as follows:

$$\overline{x}_{bw} = median + \frac{\sum_{d=1}^{n}(x_{attr,\ d,\ loc} - median)(1 - w_d^2)^2}{\sum_{d=1}^{n}(1 - w_d^2)^2} \tag{1}$$

and

$$\sigma_{bw} = \frac{\sqrt{n\ \sum_{d=1}^{n}(x_{attr,\ d,\ loc} - median)^2(1 - w_d^2)^4}}{\left|\ \sum_{d=1}^{n}(1 - w_d^2)(1 - 5w_d^2)\ \right|}, \tag{2}$$

where (i) *median* is the median of all observations $x_{attr,\ d,\ loc}$'s and (ii) w_d's are the weights. To compute w_d, let D_d denote the difference between each observation and *median* and let *medD* denote the median among all D_d's, that is, $medD = \text{median}(\{D_d \mid D_d = \text{abs}(x_{attr,\ d,\ loc} - median)\})$. Then, $w_d = \min\left\{1, \frac{c\ (x_{attr,\ d,\ loc} - median)}{medD}\right\}$ for some constant c. Although it may look more complicated to compute the bi-weight mean $\overline{x}_{bw}$ and bi-weight standard deviation σ_{bw} measures than the traditional mean $\overline{x}$ and standard deviation σ measures, it is more advantageous to use $\overline{x}_{bw}$ and σ_{bw} because they are more heavily weighted towards the centre of their distribution than outlying regions. Consequently, they are more resistant to outlying values and thus provide a more robust estimation than $\overline{x}$ and σ.

Afterwards, the temporal layer computes a standardized Z-score for each observation $x_{attr,\ d,\ loc}$ as follows:

$$\text{Z-score} = \left| \frac{x_{attr,\ d,\ loc} - \overline{x}_{bw}}{\sigma_{bw}} \right|. \tag{3}$$

Note that the *Z-score* indicates the number of standard deviation an observation is away from the mean. So, data with high Z-scores (*e.g.*, data with Z-scores > 3, which implies that the data are more than 3 standard deviations away from the mean) are identified as *suspicious data*. Users are notified so that they can check and determine whether (i) the data represent exceptions or (ii) the data are incorrect.

3.3. *The spatial layer for assuring the consistency of data with their spatial neighbours*

After showing how the internal layer checks data validity and how the temporal layer checks temporal consistency of data, let us show how the spatial layer of our CHARIOT model ensures that agro-meteorological data are consistent with their neighbours spatially. For many applications, data obtained at location *loc* are expected to be consistent with data obtained at neighbours of *loc*. Examples include (i) power and water consumption for single-family houses within the same neighbourhood, as well as (ii) temperature, rainfall and wind measures for a given region. For instance, one would expect the air temperature of New Delhi observed on a certain date to be very similar to that of its neighbouring cities/towns observed on the same date.

Hence, the challenges here are: How to ensure consistency among these spatial data? How to detect suspicious *spatial data*? How do we identify data that significantly deviate from their spatial neighbours? The spatial layer of our data quality control module answers these questions as follows. It verifies the quality of an observed datum by comparing it with data collected from surrounding areas. Although discrepancy in values between neighbours is possible, a datum should be flagged and further verified if the difference is statistically significant. The spatial layer uses the *spatial regression test*, which relies on the statistical decision theory and linear regression models to calculate a confidence interval where the data of interest are checked. To elaborate, the spatial layer applies the spatial regression test as follows. It first calculates the distances between the location of interest *loc* and each of other locations (via their coordinates). If a location loc_N lies within a user-specified radius of *loc* (*i.e.*, loc_N is located within the neighbourhood of *loc*), then loc_N is a neighbour of *loc*. For each loc_N, the spatial layer then computes the correlation (*e.g.*, Pearson's correlation) between *loc* and loc_N. Any neighbour loc_N of *loc* with significant correlation coefficient is selected. For each selected loc_N, the spatial layer generates a least-square regression line between *loc* and each qualified neighbour. For each regression line, the spatial layer calculates the root-mean-squared-error (RMSE), which is the standard deviation of the difference between the datum and the estimated least-square line value. Based on the RMSE, any observed data with values falling outside of the confidence interval range are considered as *suspicious data*. They are flagged and returned to users for further verification.

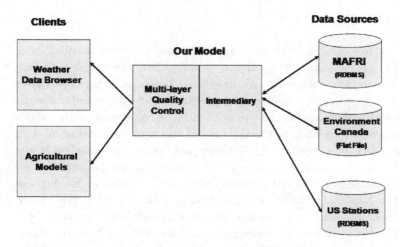

Fig. 1. Architecture of our proposed CHARIOT model.

4. Our Data Retrieval Intermediary Module

In the previous section, we described how the multi-layer data quality control module of our CHARIOT model effectively controls the quality of agro-meteorological data. In this section, let us describe another module—namely, our *data intermediary module*—used in integrating data during data retrieval from various heterogeneous database sources. This intermediary module serves dual purposes. First, it presents a standardized view of various databases wherein any differences in data formats and database structure is hidden from view. Second, it provides additional tools that address scenarios involving incompatible, missing and incomplete data.

Figure 1 shows the diagram of the location of our data intermediary module with respect to the other modules and entities in our CHARIOT model. The model consists of the data quality control module and the data intermediary module. Similar to MetBroker,[23] our model also supports data retrieval from a single station or from all stations in a geographical region across multiple databases. Our data intermediary module is directly attached to our data quality control module and is connected to different weather databases.

Recall from Section 3.2 that, during temporal data quality control, we generate a time series dataset in examining whether the datum observed on a particular date follows a consistent behaviour from historical observations. In the temporal layer, we assume that a complete time series archive of data is available. If this situation does not hold, the following strategies are taken by our intermediary:

(i) As we are dealing with data spanning the past few decades, it is highly probable that the current weather database will not contain all the datasets we need. We may need to access external archives that were stored in flat file legacy systems—database standards most applicable at that time but are not readily exchangeable with today's standards. This occurred in the case of the agro-meteorological data from MAFRI. Since the Ag-Weather program was established in the early 2000s, a complete time series dataset cannot be obtained by solely relying on MAFRI's weather database. Instead, we need to use to the National Climate Data and Information Archive from Environment Canada for obtaining historical observations. However, the archive was implemented using a legacy flat file database structure, which is incompatible with today's Manitoba Ag-Weather RDBMS. Here, the use of the intermediary of CHARIOT allows data retrieval and usage by presenting a *standardized view* of the data both from the present-day RDBMS and from legacy flat file systems. In this setting, the requesting application is not aware of how the intermediary retrieves the data. Both the query and result formats are independent of any particular implementation.

(ii) Since we are working with datasets spanning different eras and diverse geographical provenance, our current datasets may have measurement unit incompatibilities with historical datasets in keeping up with standards existing during that time. This was the case when retrieving observations from pre-1970s Canada, when the country still used the Imperial units. In the same manner, nearby stations in the US state of North Dakota still have their measurements in Imperial (*e.g.*, Fahrenheit for temperature, inches for precipitation). The intermediary module of CHARIOT takes care of this situation and has methods that automatically determine whether a unit conversion is necessary upon knowledge and verification of the time period when the data were gathered as well as the existing national measurement standard of the station where the data were observed.

(iii) Different data sources give rise to weather observations with different temporal resolutions available. For example, Manitoba Ag-Weather program currently records data in a 15-minute interval. This is not the case with older data, when we might only have records of daily highs and lows (*i.e.*, two records vs. $4 \times 24 = 96$ records). Hence, if daily data are requested but only 15-minute data are available, then our intermediary summarizes those 15-minute data to form the requested daily data before returning them for further processing.

(iv) Name changes are not uncommon (*e.g.*, Bombay in India changed its name to Mumbai). In cases where names of stations get changed, we may have a time series $TimeSeries_1$ for a station named Stn_1 prior to date d and another series $TimeSeries_2$ for a station named Stn_2 after d (where Stn_1 was renamed to Stn_2 on date d). Here, $TimeSeries_1$ and $TimeSeries_2$ are disjointed. To solve this problem, we—together with the help of domain experts who are familiar with station name changes—combine the two related time series together into one.

(v) Due to various reasons (*e.g.*, budgets, changes in agricultural activities, land development), some new weather stations may be established and some existing stations may close down. Thus, data might be unavailable for certain periods of time. For example, when a station Stn_3 is opened on date d, we only have data for this station on or after d. However, we do not have data for station Stn_3 before d. Similarly, when a station Stn_4 is closed effective on date d', we only have the data for Stn_4 on or before d' but not after d'. To solve this problem, we use data from neighbouring stations.

(vi) If a data value is missing from the time series, we apply the following sub-strategies:

(a) We perform interpolation by taking the average of the neighbouring data (*e.g.*, the previous and the next days). Weather observations that are close together (based on the date) are expected to influence each other to a greater extent than those that are far apart.

(b) We implement a data summarizing mechanism that returns to the user the available data such that decisions can be made whether or not to use the result from incomplete data values. For example, a particular request for June 21, 1960–2007 returned 98% data completeness for the time series. The missing portion (2%) does not represent a remarkable amount of observation that will skew our result, and we might as well accept this dataset for practical purposes.

(c) We assign a "threshold value" or a "grace period" to determine up to what percentage of data unavailability will be allowed before the processing is discontinued.

(vii) For cases where data are genuinely absent for the desired period and queries were not successful in returning any data, the intermediary records this absence. It keeps a log of the actual presence or absence of data in the different databases for future use. With this, the intermediary gradually "learns" from this log by allowing more seamless queries in the future, by-passing the complete execution of a query known to return an empty dataset.

During data retrieval, our intermediary sends SQL queries for relational database implementations (*e.g.*, DB2, SQL Server, Oracle), whereas file systems are accessed through direct access to the files. For each data query, we provide the intermediary with weather attributes, dates, as well as geographical locations. Then, the intermediary decides where to pass the query among the different data sources and converts it to native queries (which could then be executed by the receiving database). To effectively perform this task, the intermediary module of our CHARIOT model holds metadata for each database that serves as a *master look-up table*. Details such as weather attributes (*e.g.*, temperature, relative humidity, *etc.*), start and end dates, temporal resolution (*e.g.*, hourly, daily), station name and location (in coordinates) are provided. With this look-up table, the requesting client modules do not need to have knowledge of how data are retrieved from individual data sources, and thus are shielded away from this intricate retrieval, conversion and querying process.

5. Experimental Evaluation

We conducted various experiments, and results were consistent. For lack of space, we briefly describe the results of the following dataset. The real-time weather monitoring network consists of more than 30 weather stations. Each station collects and stores data—such as temperature, relative humidity and rainfall—at a 15-minute interval and transmits them to headquarters via a wireless network. We stored these weather data in a database running MS SQL Server and used T-SQL query scripting language to retrieve our data.

First, we compared the functionality of our CHARIOT model with related work. The following were some of the results:

- Reek *et al.*[16] proposed methods to flag conspicuous errors that discredit meteorological observations and archives. However, their methods are confined to a single station (say, only the station of interest) and fail to consider data observed at stations surrounding the station of interest. In other words, their methods do not check spatial consistency. In contrast, our CHARIOT checks data validity, temporal consistency and spatial consistency.

- The Norwegian Meteorological Institute[17] proposed methods that allow spatial data quality control of observations. The methods recommend considering 12 neighbouring stations. However, in many real-life applications, there may be more than 12 stations (say, 30 stations). The method does not provide any guidelines on which 12 out of 30 stations should be selected. Since different selections of stations may lead to different results, it is unclear how to determine the "best" selection without exhaustively examining most—if not all—of the $\binom{30}{12} > 8.64 \times 10^7$ possible selections. In contrast, our CHARIOT was designed to handle any number (whether 12 or 30) of stations.

- Instead of picking the "best" 12 stations, Kondragunta and Shrestha[18] selected all stations that fall within a 1° latitude × 1° longitude inclusion box of the station of interest. However, they check the spatial consistency *only* for rain gauge data, but *not* for other weather parameters (*e.g.*, temperature, relative humidity) which are equally important in our as well as many other real-life applications. In contrast, our CHARIOT checks various weather parameters including temperature, rainfall and relative humidity.

Then, we tested the performance of our CHARIOT model. We applied our model several times, and runtime included CPU and I/Os. Results based on the average of multiple runs show that CHARIOT was efficient. For example, the temporal layer of CHARIOT took only 4 seconds to identify suspicious temporal data on a 40-year dataset. The spatial layer of CHARIOT took about 8.2 seconds to detect suspicious spatial data when a radius of 250 km was used (*i.e.*, when considering all stations that are located within 250 km from the station of interest). Shorter runtime was required when the radius of neighbourhood was shorter. Table 1 shows how runtime decreased when the radius decreased.

Table 1.   Runtime of CHARIOT when the radius of the neighbourhood varies.

Radius of the neighbourhood	Runtime
50 km	1.0 seconds
100 km	2.2 seconds
150 km	3.8 seconds
200 km	5.9 seconds
250 km	8.2 seconds

Next, we evaluated the accuracy and effectiveness of our CHARIOT model in controlling the quality of data. We randomly seeded several abnormal (*e.g.*, those exceeding limits, those temporally or spatially different from their nearby values) as well as normal observations into our dataset. We tested whether CHARIOT detects all suspicious observations. Fig. 2 shows the precision and recall of CHARIOT. The x-axis of the figure shows the percentage of observations that were seeded (*e.g.*, 10% of seeded observations mean that 90% of observations in the dataset were original and 10% were seeded). The y-axis of Fig. 2(a) shows precision, while that of Fig. 2(b) shows recall. In both graphs, when the percentage of seeded observations increased (*i.e.*, more seeded observations), the number of abnormal observations (to be detected) also increased. Hence, both precision and recall decreased. Moreover, when the number of standard deviation used for Z-scores (and for confidence interval) increased, abnormal observations lie relatively closer to the normal ones. Hence, both precision and recall decreased. Nonetheless, it is important to note that both precision and recall of CHARIOT were very high (with precision > 88% and recall > 92%). Almost all of the detected/flagged observations were abnormal, and almost all of the abnormal observations were detected. In other words, the number of false positives and the number of false negatives were very low.

Finally, we applied two datasets to a data mining engine for agricultural applications (*e.g.*, weather prediction). The first dataset was the original dataset. We fed this original dataset into our CHARIOT model. Some observations were detected and flagged (by any of three layers in our system) and returned to us. After further investigation, we removed those invalid and/or incorrect observations and kept those truly exceptional observations. The resulting dataset became the second dataset for this experiment. Experimental results show that the second dataset led to more useful data mining results (*e.g.*, more accurate weather prediction) when compared with the first dataset. This shows the effectiveness of our proposed model.

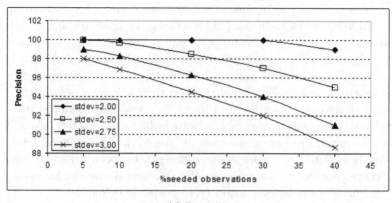

(a) Precision

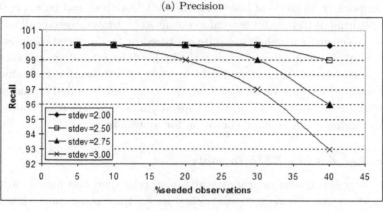

(b) Recall

Fig. 2. Precision and recall

6. Discussion

In previous sections, we illustrated the applicability and the effectiveness of our proposed CHARIOT model for applications in agro-meteorology. In this section, let us discuss the generalizability of our model and its applications in areas other than agro-meteorology, as well as the future of weather databases in XML.

6.1. *Generalizability of our CHARIOT model*

CHARIOT can be applied in diversified areas such as (i) utility consumption monitoring, (ii) pest and insect control, as well as (iii) law enforcement. For utility consumption monitoring, we can apply CHARIOT to ensure that the readings from power, gas or water meters are valid and within their reasonable range. In addition, CHARIOT can be used to check if each household follows a consistent consumption pattern with respect to a yearly cycle (*e.g.*, higher heating consumption during the winter months). Utility companies could then use the results in detecting malfunctioning meters and advising customers on unusual changes in their utility consumption.

Moreover, CHARIOT can be used in a city's mosquito count surveillance and control measures program to ensure public health safety brought about by mosquito-borne ailments such as West Nile and dengue fever. A significantly elevated mosquito count difference between a locality and others alerts authorities to target a specific area and apply the necessary measures for insect population control (*e.g.*, pesticide defogging).

Furthermore, in the field of law enforcement, CHARIOT can be applied to the monitoring of traffic and law enforcement in highways. Specifically, it can be used to ensure the validity of data captured by traffic speed cameras; it can also help pinpoint which sectors of the highway have an abnormal rate of traffic violations or an increased vehicle passage rate leading to traffic jams and congestions. Law enforcement agencies can then be aided in taking the appropriate actions such as adjusting speed limits and re-routing traffic, while maintaining a safe driving condition for motorists.

6.2. *Weather data in XML formats*

So far, we have illustrated weather databases in relational and flat-file formats as well as the different compatibility issues that accompany them. Here, let us discuss a trend, which we think weather databases would be taking as a standard in the future—towards XML.

XML facilitates data exchange and storage. Representing weather data in XML makes the data available not only in machine-readable but also in a human readable self-describing form. Unlike existing relational databases, XML formats make the data representation independent of any computing platform and database vendor. It is important to note that weather databases in XML are largely disseminated to the public via the Internet. As an additional benefit, having XML weather databases opens weather data to be accessed in portable electronic devices such as mobile phones. It will allow farmers to have mobile access on important agro-meteorological decision support tools while in the field. Recently, some national weather bureaux, such as the US National Weather Service, have started providing weather data in an open-access XML format known as the National Digital Forecast Database (NDFD). A variety of weather parameters are contained in the NDFD XML weather database such as maximum, minimum, hourly and dew point temperatures, precipitation amount, wind direction, as well as speed. As weather databases gear toward XML as the standard, another set of compatibility issues would arise with current and historical data representation during collaborative data exchange and usage. However, unlike legacy flat file systems, portability issues are kept to a minimum as conversion tools are readily available.

7. Conclusions

Weather plays an important role in many activities, particularly in agriculture. Accurate weather information is important as many agricultural decision support tools rely on weather data as their inputs. However, the accuracy of this information as well as the output of these tools depends upon the quality of data. In addition, weather data collected throughout the years are heterogeneous and incompatible. In this paper, we developed (i) an *intermediary module* that successfully integrates data from diverse weather data sources and (ii) an effective three-layer *data quality control module*. Our intermediary solves compatibility issues among incompatible weather data brought about by differences on format, national standards and data resolution. Our data quality control module consists of three layers. The internal layer ensures that observed data are valid and fall within their ranges. The temporal layer ensures that data are consistent with their temporal behaviour in the time series, and the spatial layer ensures that data observed at a certain location are consistent with its spatial neighbours. Experimental results on real-life data collected from a network of 30 weather stations in the province of Manitoba in Canada showed the effectiveness of our CHARIOT model. Specifically, it showed that our intermediary successfully integrated weather data from diverse sources, and that the use of our data quality control module for agro-meteorological data led to more accurate agricultural decision support tools. It is important to note that the applicability of CHARIOT is not confined to agro-meteorology. CHARIOT is also applicable in other diversified application domains as well.

Acknowledgments

This project is partially supported by (i) Manitoba Agriculture, Food and Rural Initiatives (MAFRI), (ii) Manitoba Centre of Excellence Fund (MCEF), (iii) Mathematics of Information Technology and Complex Systems (MITACS) in the Canadian Networks of Centres of Excellence

(NCE), (iv) Natural Sciences and Engineering Research Council of Canada (NSERC), and (v) The University of Manitoba. Special thanks to Andrew J. Nadler, an agro-meteorologist from MAFRI, for his domain knowledge and expertise.

References

1. J. R. Wallin, Summary of recent progress in predicting late blight epidemics in United States and Canada, *American Potato J.* **39**, pp. 306–312 (1962).
2. C. Robinson and N. Mort, A neural network system for the protection of citrus crops from frost damage, *Computers and Electronics in Agriculture* **16**(3), pp. 177–187 (1997).
3. M. Benedikt, P. Bohannon and G. Bruns, Data cleaning for decision support, in *Proc. CleanDB 2006*.
4. G. Cong, W. Fan, *et al.*, Improving data quality: consistency and accuracy, in *Proc. VLDB 2007*, pp. 315–326.
5. B. T. Dai, N. Koudas, *et al.*, Column heterogeneity as a measure of data quality, in *Proc. CleanDB 2006*.
6. M. Helfert and C. Herrmann, Proactive data quality management for data warehouse systems: a metadata based data quality system, in *Proc. DMDW 2002*, pp. 97–106.
7. D. P. Ballou and H. L. Pazer, Modeling data and process quality in multi-input, multi-output information systems, *Management Science* **31**(2), pp. 150–162 (1985).
8. T. C. Redman, *Data Quality: The Field Guide* (Digital Press, Newton, MA, USA, 2001).
9. R. W. Wang and D. M. Strong, Beyond accuracy: what data quality means to data consumers, *J. Management Information Systems* **12**(4), pp. 5–35 (1996).
10. W. Du, Ensuring data consistency in large network systems, in *Proc. DASFAA 2001*, pp. 336–343.
11. K. G. Hubbard, S. Goddard, *et al.*, Performance of quality assurance procedures for an applied climate information system, *J. Atmospheric and Oceanic Technology* **22**, pp. 105–112 (2005).
12. S. Karatas and L. Yalcin, Data quality management, in *Proc. TECO 2005*.
13. P. Missier, S. Embury, *et al.*, Quality views: capturing and exploiting the user perspective on data quality, in *Proc. VLDB 2006*, pp. 977–988.
14. S. W. Sadiq, M. E. Orlowska, *et al.*, Induction of data quality protocols into business process management, in *Proc. ICEIS 2007*, Vol. DISI, pp. 473–476.
15. J. You and K. G. Hubbard, Quality control of weather data during extreme events, *J. Atmospheric and Oceanic Technology* **23**(2), pp. 184–197 (2006).
16. T. Reek, S. R. Doty, *et al.*, A deterministic approach to the validation of historical daily temperature and precipitation data from the cooperative network, *Bulletin of the American Meteorological Society* **73**(6), pp. 753–762 (1992).
17. F. Vejen (ed.), C. Jacobsson, *et al.*, *Quality Control of Meteorological Ob-*

servations: Automatic Methods Used in the Nordic Countries, Report 8/2002 KLIMA, Norwegian Meteorological Institute (Oslo, Norway, 2002).

18. C. R. Kondragunta and K. Shrestha, Automated real-time operational rain gauge quality-control tools in NWS hydrologic operations, in *Proc. 20th American Meteorological Society Conf. on Hydrology* (2006).

19. C. K.-S. Leung, M. A. F. Mateo and A. J. Nadler, CAMEL: an intelligent computational model for agro-meteorological data, in *Proc. ICMLC 2007*, pp. 1960–1965.

20. C. K.-S. Leung, M. A. F. Mateo and A. J. Nadler, An effective multi-layer model for controlling the quality of data, in *Proc. IDEAS 2007*, pp. 28–36.

21. C. K.-S. Leung, R. K. Thulasiram and D. A. Bondarenko, An efficient system for detecting outliers from financial time series, in *Proc. BNCOD 2006*, pp. 190–198.

22. J. Lanzante, Resistant, robust and non-parametric techniques for the analysis of climate data: theory and examples, including applications to historical radiosonde station data, *Int. J. Climatology* **16**(11), pp. 1197–1226 (1996).

23. M. R. Laurenson, T. Kiura and S. Ninomiya, Providing agricultural models with mediated access to heterogeneous weather databases, *Applied Engineering in Agriculture* **18**(5), pp. 617–625 (2002).

42

Assessing Data Quality Within Available Context*

Jingyu Han*

*Nanjing University of Posts and Telecommunications,
Nanjing, 210003, China*
* E-mail:hjysky@gmail.com

Dawei Jiang

Southeast University, Nanjing, 210096, China
E-mail:davidjiang2005@gmail.com

Zhiming Ding

Institute of Software, Chinese Academy of Science, Beijing, 100080, China
E-mail:zhiming@iscas.ac.cn

Data quality rating is an important issue to be considered in many scenarios such as data integration, cooperative information system(CIS) . Now it is widely accepted that data quality can be measured from multiple dimensions such as accuracy,completeness etc. Most of the work focuses on how to qualitatively analyze the dimensions and the analysis will greatly depend on experts' knowledge.Seldom work is given on how to automatically quantify data quality dimensions. To solve this challenging problem,we propose a novel approach to automatically Quantify Dimensions within Context(QDC). Data quality can be gauged by discrepancy between data view and its entity's perfect representation.Since it is difficult to obtain the perfect representation of entity, we propose to approximate the perfect representation within its available context and quality dimensions can be quantified in this context scope. By naturally borrowing entropy concepts from information theory, the measurement is easily given for different types of data. In this way the two most import quality dimensions,that are accuracy and completeness, are properly quantified. Our QDC approach can not only give an objective score and ranking in a cooperative multi-source environment but also avoid human's laborious interaction. As an automatic quality rating solution our approach is distinguished , especially for large scale datasets.Theory and experiment shows our approach performs well for quality rating.

---

*The work was partially supported by the National Natural Science Foundation of China under Grant No. 60573164 , and by SRF for ROCS, SEM

1. Introduction

Data Quality is a problem as follows. Given a set of data sources which describe the same entities, we are to give each record or each data source in the data sources a numerical score which indicates how *good* of that record or data source with regard to its corresponding entity under certain measurements such as accuracy and completeness. This problem is a fundamental problem in a number of domains, including data integration, data warehouse, and distributed databases.

Solving the Data Quality problem in a Cooperative Information System (CIS) is a pressing concern.[3,13] A CIS is an information system that interconnects an amount of data sources. These data sources are independently developed and represent the same entities.[9] For example,in an e-government scenario public administrations,citizen bureaus and enterprises all have the data related to citizens. In such systems, it is important to figure out which record or data source is *good* or not in that the data sources are independently built and many unintentional errors such as typos and misspellings often occurred in the development. The *goodness* of a data source can be measured in terms of many dimensions, including accuracy, completeness, consistency, minimality and timeliness.[1,10] In this paper, we focus on the *accuracy* and *completeness* since they are the most importance measurements.

A possible way to solve above problem is to invite a human expert to identify the *perfect representation* for each entity. Then, the accuracy and completeness can be measured by the distance between each record with its perfect representation based on some distance function such as Euclidean Distance and Edit Distance. Unfortunately, this approach does not scale well for large CIS systems since it introduces *huge* human efforts. Furthermore, the Euclidean or Edit distance can not be directly applied to both numerical and text data. To obtain a good ranking of these types of data, people usually use ad hoc ways to compare them. Thus,it is a necessity to find a universal measurement to quantify the similarity of both numerical and text data.

In this paper, we propose a novel Data Quality scheme for CIS systems. We call our approach Quantify Dimensions within Context (QDC). The novelty of our approach is that our approach *automatically* rank each record or data source a score with *little* human efforts.

Our idea is based on the following observations. *First*, in real CIS systems, the same entity are often redundantly stored in many data sources. Although each data source in CIS is independently maintained and unintentional errors often occurr during the development, it is not likely that all the copies of the same entity are simultaneously wrong. We propose that the *perfect representation* can be approximated among all the data sources when accuracy is measured and that the *most complete* representation can also be synthesized when completeness is measured. This is a feasible solution to quantify quality scores. *Second,*we observe that information entropy can naturally reflect how much useful information is conveyed by data and thus dimensions can be quantified based on this terms. This will give birth to a universal quantitive measurement for different types of data such as text and numerical data. Based on above observations, our QDC approach works as follows.

Step 1: By mapping each record or data source into a hash space, the *context* of each record or data source will be identified. It can provides the available records or data sources to be compared with.

Step 2: In *context*, the *most approximation* of each record or data source is synthesized by vote-fusion policy, which acts as the substitution of entity's perfect representation.

Step 3: *Accuracy* is measured by comparing data with the *most approximation* based on Information Entropy. *Completeness* is measured by comparing data with all the *context* members based on Information Entropy.

We make the following contributions.

- In practice the perfect representation is unavailable or even available,the cost will be too large. We propose that quality references can be derived from its available context and thus data quality can be *automatically* evaluated without human interaction. This is the greatest advantage of our approach, especially for large data sources.
- Borrowing entropy concept from information theory, the measurement of *accuracy* and *completeness* can be intuitively determined for different types of data.
- By mapping data into a hash space our algorithm can scale well with the size of data source. Theory and experiment shows that our approach has a good performance.

The paper is organized as follows. Section 2 reviews related work. Section 3 presents the problem setting and devotes to the details of QDC. Section 4 empirically validate the effectiveness of the proposed QDC approach, followed by conclusion and future work in Section 5.

2.   Related Work

The research on quality evaluations can be separated into two large categories.[11] The first category focus on *qualitatively* analyzing data quality dimensions.[1,7,8,10] Literature Ref. 1 analyzes data quality from four dimensions: accuracy, completeness, consistency and minimality, which have been widely accepted now. But the quality evaluation will greatly depend on human assistance. In literature Ref. 7 a requirement analysis methodology is developed to specify the tags needed to estimate, determine and enhance data quality. Data quality is defined in terms of quality parameters and quality indicators. The former is qualitative and subjective information, while the latter provides objective information about data. Literature Ref. 8 gives a thorough analysis of freshness dimension. Literature Ref. 10 bases data quality dimensions on ontology and an information system is perceived as a representation of an application domain. It only gives theoretical analysis of quality dimensions based on ontology, but it does not give how to quantitatively estimate these dimensions. Some work evaluate quality in terms of user's requirements.[2,6,25] Here data quality is defined as fitness for use, i.e, the ability to meet user's requirements and the user's quality requirement should be specified in the data processing environment. Above research mainly gives what data quality means and how to measure data quality qualitatively, but it will be needed to ask people to give the rating or tags. This is too laborious and even impossible for large dataset.

The second category deals with how to *quantitatively* rate quality dimensions and it mainly aims at relational data.[4,5,22] A.Parssian gives a method to estimate accuracy an completeness in terms of tuple level for relational data. In turn it is analysed how these two dimensions will affect primitive relational algebra operations.[4,22] A.Motro Ref. 5 gives an approach on how to rate soundness and completeness of relational data. To avoid the human authentication,statistical (essentially,sampling) method is exploited to keep the manual work within acceptable limits. The shortcoming of these approaches is that the manual verification is very laborious. In fact, it is not a good policy and it is infeasible for large datasets. Donald P.Ballou propose to estimate query result quality by sampling from base tables.[23] Of course,it will not reflect the dataset's quality accurately.

The work closely related to us is how to assess data quality in Cooperative Information System(CIS). In literature Ref. 15, a methodological framework for data quality in cooperative systems has been proposed, consisting of five phases (i.e., definition,measurement,exchange,analysis and improvement). DaQuinCIS Refs. 3,12,16 is also a platform to address interoperability in CIS. In this framework, each organization exports data with XML-based quality data avoiding dissemination of low quality data in CIS. But they do not give how to pinpoint the standard against which data quality can be gauged and how to effectively quantify quality objectively in CIS.

3. Quantifying Dimensions within Context

3.1. *Problem Setting*

We first define an abstract Cooperative Information System as follows.

Definition 3.1. Given a set of entities $E = \{e_1, \ldots, e_n\}$, a Cooperative Information System (CIS) is N data sources $D = \{T_1, \ldots, T_N\}$ which store E as follows. Each data source $T_i \in D$ contains a lot of records, i.e., $T_i = \{r_1, \ldots, r_n\}$ and each record $r_i \in T_i$ is a copy of e_i with unexpected modifications such as missing attribute values, or misspellings.

Please note that the exact representation of each entity e_i is often not known in the CIS since we can only obtain its modified copies stored in the data sources. The goal of a Data Quality scheme is to give each record r_i or data source T_i a numerical score to indicate the goodness r_i or T_i regarding to e_i or E, respectively.

In a CIS, we assume that the schema mapping between the data sources is available. If it is not the case, the schema mapping can be obtained by many schema mapping techniques Ref. 18,19 and data profiling tools Ref. 20,21.

3.2. *Extracting Most Approximation of Record and Data Source*

To solve the Data Quality problem in CIS, our approach consists of two steps. In the first step, we extract the most approximation for each record r_i, denoted as r_i', or data source T_i, denoted at T_i'. In the second step, we develop an Information Theory based method to measure the accuracy and completeness of r_i and T_i. This subsection presents the first step. Calculating accuracy and completeness is discussed in the next two subsections respectively.

Given a record r_i, although the exact (perfect) representation of its corresponding entity e_i is not available, we have pointed out in Section 1 that a number of copies of e_i (including r_i) are stored in D and we can approximate the representation of e_i from its redundant copies.

This is done in two steps. First, we collect *similar* records of r_i and regard all the similar records (including r_i) as a *context* of r_i. Then, we use a fusion-voting algorithm to extract most approximation of r_i from the *context* of r_i. We will describe the methods and algorithms in detail.

Definition 3.2. With specific similarity measurement $sim(\cdot, \cdot)$ and threshold θ_r, context of a record r_i is

$$con(r_i) = \{r_j | sim(r_i, r_j) > \theta_r, r_j \in T_j, j = 1, \ldots, N\} \qquad (1)$$

We define the context of r_i is the collection of records which are similar to r_i with similarity threshold greater than θ_r. Given a pair of records (r_i, r_j) with m common attributes, the similarity between them is defined as Jaro similarity and calculated as follows.

$$sim(r_i, r_j) = Jaro(r_i, r_j) = \frac{1}{m} \sum_{k=1}^{m} \frac{|G_n(r_i[k]) \cap G_n(r_j[k])|}{|G_n(r_i[k]) \cup G_n(r_j[k])|} \qquad (2)$$

where $r_i[k]$ denotes the value of k-th attribute of r_i and $G_n(r_i[k])$ is the n-gram representation multiset of $r_i[k]$. n-gram representation of a string S is defined in Definition 3.3 Ref. 17. If $r_i[k]$ is a numerical data, we also convert it into a n-gram hash space based on fixed interval and here n-gram is a range of intervals.

Definition 3.3. Let S be a string of length p, denoted as $l_1 l_2, \ldots, l_p (p > n)$. It contains $p - n + 1$ *n-grams* and each n-gram is a substring constituted by n continuous letters. The multiset of n-grams S contains is denoted as $G_n(S)$.

For example, string 'abcdab' contains five 2-grams, G_2('abcdab')={ 'ab'.2, 'bc'.1, 'cd'.1, 'da'.1 }. String 'abcda' has four 2-grams G_2('abcda')={ 'ab'.1, 'bc'.1, 'cd'.1 , 'da'.1 }. It is obvious that

$$Jaro(G_2('abcdab'), G_2('abcda')) = 4/5. \qquad (3)$$

When the context of r_i is identified, the most approximation r_i' with regard to e_i is extracted from $con(r_i)$. To to this, we adopt a voting-fusion policy Ref. 14. That is to say, voting for r_i' is based on occurrences in the context because identical answers tend to reinforce the likelihood of their value being correct. Alg.3.1 and Alg.3.2 depict the algorithms for identifying the context of r_i and extracting r_i'.

Algorithm 3.1. *identifyRecordContext*

Input r_i ,$D=\{T_1, T_2, \ldots, T_N\}$ *and similarity threshold* θ_r
Output $con(r_i)$
Begin
  $con(r_i) \leftarrow \Phi$
  for $j \leftarrow 1; j \leq N; j \neq i$ **do**
    $maxSim \leftarrow 0;$
    $r^{maxSim} \leftarrow null;$
    while *not end of* T_j **do**
      compute $Jaro(r_i, r_m)(r_m \in T_j);$
      if $(Jaro(r_i, r_m) \geq \theta_r) \wedge ((Jaro(r_i, r_m) \geq r^{maxSim})$ **then**
        replace r^{maxSim} *with* $r_m;$
      end
    end
    $con(r_i) \leftarrow con(r_i) \cup \{r^{maxSim}\};$
  end
  return $con(r_i);$
End

Algorithm 3.2. *voteMostApprRecord*

Input $con(r_i)$ *and* θ_{sam}
Output *most approximation* r_i'
Begin
  for $i \leftarrow 1$ **to** $|con(r_i)|$ **do**
    for $k \leftarrow 1$ **to** m **do**
      Map $r_i[k]$ *into n-gram space and calculate* $G_n(r_i[k]);$
    end
  end
  $sameRecordNumArray[|con(r_i)|] \leftarrow \{0, 0, \ldots, 0\};$
  $maxNum \leftarrow 1;$
  $mostApprRecordIndex \leftarrow 1;$
  for $i \leftarrow 1$ **to** $|con(r_i)|$
    for $j \leftarrow 1$ **to** $|con(r_i)|$ **do**
      $Jaro(r_i, r_j) \leftarrow \frac{1}{m} \sum_{k=1}^{m} Jaro(r_i[k], r_j[k]);$
      if $Jaro(r_i, r_j) \geq \theta_{sam}$ **then**
        $sameRecordNumArray[i]++;$
      end
    end
    if $sameRecordNumArray[i] \geq maxNum$ **then**

$\qquad maxNum \leftarrow sameRecordNumArray[i];$
$\qquad mostApprRecordIndex \leftarrow i;$
$\quad$ **end**
end
$r'_i \leftarrow r_{mostApprRecordIndex};$
return $r'_i;$
End

The notions of context and approximate representations can be generalized to the data source level.

Definition 3.4. With specific similarity metric sim and threshold θ_T , context of a data source T_i is

$$con(T_i) = \{T_j | sim(T_i, T_j) > \theta_T, j = 1, \ldots, N\} \qquad (4)$$

The similarity between T_i and T_j is calculated as two steps. First, compute the similarity for a common attribute k of T_i and T_j.

$$sim(T_i[k], T_j[k]) = Jaro(T_i[k], T_j[k]) = \frac{|G_n(T_i[k]) \cap G_n(T_j[k])|}{|G_n(T_i[k]) \cup G_n(T_j[k])|} \qquad (5)$$

where $T_i[k]$ is the concatenation of k-th attribute values of all the records in T_i.

Then, the similarity of two different data sources T_i, T_j with k common attributes is calculated as

$$sim(T_i, T_j) = \frac{1}{m} \sum_{k=1}^{m} sim(T_i[k], T_j[k]). \qquad (6)$$

The context $con(T_i)$ is calculated by Alg.3.3. As for most approximation T'_i of T_i,the ideal one will be a combination of most approximations with regard to each entity e_i from different data sources. To get most approximation of one entity e_i,the records in all data sources in D will be compared with. So,it is too costly to get all the most approximations for all entities and even unaffordable for large scale data sources. Thus we calculate most approximation T'_i according to Alg.3.4.

Algorithm 3.3. *identifyDataSourceContext*

Input T_i , $D = \{T_1, T_2, \ldots, T_N\}$ *and similarity threshold* θ_T
Output $con(T_i)$
Begin
  $con(T_i) \leftarrow \Phi$;
  Each attribute of T_i *is mapped into n-gram space,*
  denoted as $G_n(T_i[k])(1 \leq k \leq m)$;
  for $j \leftarrow 1; j \leq N; j \neq i$ **do**
    $accSim \leftarrow 0$;
    for $k \leftarrow 1$ **to** m
      map $T_j[k]$ *into n-gram space, denoted as* $G_n(T_j[k])$;
      $accSim \leftarrow accSim + \frac{|G_n(T_i[k]) \cap G_n(T_j[k])|}{|G_n(T_i[k]) \cup G_n(T_j[k])|}$;
    end
    if $\frac{1}{m} accSim \geq \theta_T$ **then**
      $con(T_i) \leftarrow con(T_i) \cup \{T_j\}$;
    end
  end
  return $con(T_i)$;
End

Algorithm 3.4. *voteMostApprDataSource*

Input $con(T_i)$ *and* θ_{sam}
Output *most approximation* T_i'
Begin
  for $i \leftarrow 1$ **to** u **do**
    for $k \leftarrow 1$ **to** m **do**
      Map $T_i[k]$ *into n-gram space and calculate* $G_n(T_i[k])$;
    end
  end
  $sameDataSourceNumArray[m] \leftarrow \{0, 0, \ldots, 0\}$;
  $maxNum \leftarrow 1$;
  $mostApprDataSourceIndex \leftarrow 1$;
  for $i \leftarrow 1$ **to** u **do**
    for $j \leftarrow 1$ **to** u **do**
      $Jaro(T_i, T_j) \leftarrow \frac{1}{m} \sum_{k=1}^{m} Jaro(T_i[k], T_j[k])$;
      if $Jaro(T_i, T_j) \geq \theta_{sam}$ **then**
        $sameDataSourceNumArray[i]++$;
    end
  end

if $sameDataSourceNumArray[i] \geq maxNum$ **then**
  $maxNum \leftarrow sameDataSourceNumArray[i];$
  $mostApprDataSourceIndex \leftarrow i;$
  end
end
$T_i' \leftarrow T_{mostApprDataSourceIndex};$
return $T_i';$
End

3.3. Accuracy Measurement

Thus far, we have described how to identify the context and most approximation of record r_i and data source T_i. In this subsection, we will describe how to compute accuracy for r_i and T_i within their contexts.

The accuracy is determined based on the methods of Information Theory. We first introduce two Information Theory concepts.

Definition 3.5. Given a multiset X with its members' occurrence frequency $P(X)$, entropy of X is defined as

$$H(X) = -\sum_X P(x) \lg P(x) \tag{7}$$

where $\lg P(x)$ is a logarithmic function with base 2.

Definition 3.6. Given two distributions $p(X)$ and $q(X)$, differential entropy is defined as

$$D(p\|q) = \sum_X p(x) \lg p(x) - \sum_X p(x) \lg q(x) \tag{8}$$

3.3.1. Measure Accuracy at Record Level

Accuracy of r_i may be measured by the information proximity between r_i and r_i'. It is defined as follows

$$acc(r_i) = \frac{||H(G_n(r_i))| - |D(G_n(r_i')||G_n(r_i))||}{|H(G_n(r_i))|}. \tag{9}$$

Confidence of $acc(r_i)$ is defined as formula

$$conf(acc(r_i)) = \frac{\sum_{i=1}^{u} \frac{1}{2^i}}{\sum_{i=1}^{N} \frac{1}{2^i}}. \tag{10}$$

Here u is the number of members in $con(r_i)$. It implies that the larger the context is, the sure we are of the accuracy obtained.It can be seen that the marginal certainty obtained by every more member of context is decreasing.

3.3.2. *Measure Accuracy at Data Source Level*

Accuracy of T_i may be measured by the information proximity between T_i and T_i'. It is defined as follows

$$acc(T_i) = \frac{||H(G_n(T_i))| - |D(G_n(T_i')||G_n(T_i))||}{|H(G_n(T_i))|}. \tag{11}$$

Confidence of $acc(T_i)$ is defined as formula

$$conf(acc(T_i)) = \frac{\sum_{i=1}^{u} \frac{1}{2^i}}{\sum_{i=1}^{N} \frac{1}{2^i}}. \tag{12}$$

Here u is the number of members in $con(T_i)$.

3.4. *Completeness Measurement*

In this subsection, we will describe how to determine completeness for record r_i and data source T_i.

3.4.1. *Measure Completeness at Record Level*

The larger the number of members in $con(r_i)$ is, the more information data source will contain. In other words,$con(r_i)$ will contain more information than any member in $con(r_i)$. Thus, completeness can be gauged by the ratio of information conveyed by r_i to that conveyed by $con(r_i)$. Average information conveyed by r_i is

$$H(r_i) = \frac{1}{m} \sum_{k=1}^{m} H(G_n(r_i[k])). \tag{13}$$

The average information conveyed by $con(r_i)$ is

$$H(con(r_i)) = \frac{1}{m} \sum_{k=1}^{m} H(G_n(r_1[k]) \cup G_n(r_2[k] \cup \ldots \cup G_n(r_u[k]))). \tag{14}$$

Thus we can get the completeness of r_i as follows

$$comp(r_i) = \frac{H(r_i)}{H(con(r_i))}. \tag{15}$$

Confidence of $comp(r_i)$ may be similarly defined as before.

3.4.2. *Measure Completeness at Data Source Level*

Completeness can be gauged by the ratio of information conveyed by T_i to that conveyed by $con(T_i)$. Average information conveyed by T_i is

$$H(T_i) = \frac{1}{m} \sum_{k=1}^{m} H(G_n(T_i[k])) \,. \tag{16}$$

The average information conveyed by $con(T_i)$ is

$$H(con(T_i)) = \frac{1}{m} \sum_{k=1}^{m} H(G_n(T_1[k]) \cup G_n(T_2[k] \cup \ldots \cup G_n(T_u[k]))) \,. \tag{17}$$

Thus we can get the completeness of T_i as follows

$$comp(T_i) = \frac{H(T_i)}{H(con(T_i))} \,. \tag{18}$$

Confidence of $comp(T_i)$ can also be similarly determined as before.

4. Experiments

Since there is no general benchmark to test data quality until now, we experiment on synthetic data source where we can easily control the perfect representations of all the entities. The synthetic data sources are produced as narrated next.The perfect representation data source is obtained from globalcomputing[a] which contains five attributes {Name,Municipality,Address,County,Population}. It acts as E(the whole set of e_i) with 36,000 community entities. Eight synthetic data sources,that are $\{T_1, T_2, \ldots, T_8\}$ are produced by copying record by record from E according to such three rules.

(1) Each record is copied from E to destination data sources and α % percentage of the eight data sources will be filled .

(2) When records are scattered from E to $T_i(1 \leq i \leq 8)$, they will be transferred without any changes $\beta\%$ percentage of times .

(3) When a record is scattered into destination data sources introducing errors, $\gamma\%$ percentage of copies will be affected with one of the six operations: *letter insertion,letter deletion,letter substitution,numerical range change(10%),cell null* and *record duplication.*

Parameter Used

α	β	γ
0.875	0.80	0.70

---

[a]http://www.globalcomputing.com

With above parameters, the D is produced and the number of records in each data source varies from 29855 to 34078.

Since E is the perfect representations of all the entities,the real accuracy and completeness can be obtained by brute force. Suppose that $r_i \in T_i$ is a record of T_i and its corresponding perfect entity is e,then its real accuracy and completeness is as follows.

$$acc_{real}(r_i) = \frac{||H(G_n(r_i))| - |D(G_n(e)||G_n(r_i))||}{|H(r_i)|} \qquad (19)$$

$$comp_{real}(r_i) = \frac{|H(G_n(r_i))|}{|H(e)|} \qquad (20)$$

To get accuracy of $T_i(1 \leq i \leq 8)$, each record of T_i will be compared with all the records in E to test whether it is the same with some record in E. In other words,real accuracy of T_i is

$$acc_{real}(T_i) = \frac{|H(G_n(T_i \cap E))|}{|H(G_n(T_i))|} \qquad (21)$$

Real completeness of T_i is

$$comp_{real}(T_i) = \frac{|H(G_n(T_i \cap E))|}{|H(G_n(E))|} \qquad (22)$$

Since in a cooperative multi-source environment people are usually interested in the top k records or data sources regarding to accuracy and completeness ,we will adopt the top k coverage measurement,denoted as cov_k. It is obtained by the following steps.[24]

Step 1: The scores returned by brute force and QDC will be ranked by descending order.

Step 2: The top k ones by brute force and QDC will be denoted as top_k^{real} and top_k^{QDC}.

Step 3: The top k coverage is defined as follows.

$$cov_k = \frac{|top_k^{real} \cap top_k^{QDC}|}{|top_k^{real}|} \qquad (23)$$

Here top_k^{real} is the top k ones in terms of real accuracy or completeness and top_k^{QDC} is the top k ones in terms of accuracy or completeness,which is obtained by QDC approach. In our experiment k varies from 1 to the half total number of context data sources.

4.1. *Measurement at Record Level*

In this scenario,accuracy and completeness of each record is calculated based on *identifyRecordContext* and *voteMostApprRecord* algorithms. We test 10 times. Each time we randomly select 100 records among eight data sources and compute the average cov_k. The figure 1 aims at accuracy measurement and the figure 2 aims at completeness measurement.

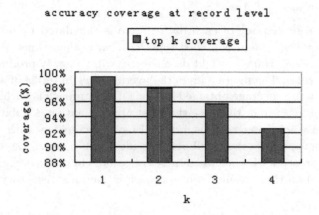

Fig. 1. Coverage of Accuracy at Record Level

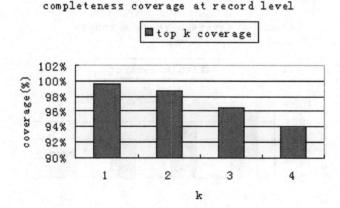

Fig. 2. Coverage of Completeness at Record Level

It shows that our QDC approach has a high top k coverage and the coverage is 93% at worst. It also shows that the larger k is,the coverage will

be lower. We think the reason is as follows. The ranking is deter minded
by the scores and each score is computed by comparing itself with the
synthesized one within context. Thus,the larger the gap is,the larger the
error will also be.

4.2. *Measurement at Data Source Level*

4.2.1. *Performance of Accuracy*

In this scenario,accuracy of each data source is calculated by our *identifyDataSourceContext* and *voteMostApprDataSource* algorithms. We tested
10 times and every time the eight data sources will be newly produced with
above three rules. The figure 3 gives the average cov_k in terms of accuracy.
It shows that the coverage obtained by our QDC approach is within an acceptable limits. Since in this case the most approximation is a data source
selected as a whole,some records in it will have discrepancy with true values. Since unexpected errors will occur randomly in a sense, the cov_k will
be stable no matter whether the number of records in data sources is large
or not. Based on these results, our approach is overall satisfactory.

4.2.2. *Performance of Completeness*

In this scenario, completeness of each data source is calculated mainly based
on our *identifyDataSourceContext*.

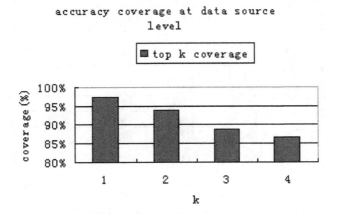

Fig. 3.   Coverage of Accuracy at Data Source Level

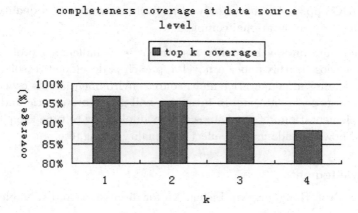

Fig. 4.   Coverage of Completeness at Data Source Level

The figure 4 gives the average cov_k in terms of completeness. It shows the completeness by our QDC approach gives an acceptable result. But due to the unexpected errors the distribution of context will always be distorted from E,the gap will also always exists.

The state of the art about quantifying data quality is sample-based combined with human iteration,[4,5] while our work is an *automatic* approach. It is unfair to compare QDC approach with them and we will not do this again.

5. Conclusions

In this paper, we propose that quality should be assessed in its available context scope and data quality implies how much information may be conveyed by data. Based on this insight a context-based quality estimation approach is developed. The meaning of this paper can be summarized as follows.

- Since data quality can be gauged by discrepancy between data and its entity's perfect representation, we propose that data quality can be feasibly gauged by discrepancy between data and the synthesized one in context instead. This is the key of quantifying quality *automatically*.
- Data quality is closely related to its available context and different context will lead to different rating for the same data set. Although the larger the context scope is, the more sure we are of the rating. In practice, with a reasonable context an acceptable quality rating can usually be obtained.

- Our QDC approach can not only objectively measures data quality but also has low computational complexity.

To sum up, automatic quality assessment is a challenging problem in many scenarios. In this paper a novel approach is developed to solve this problem. It aims at cooperative multi-source environment and is especially useful in large scale datasets. In future we will give a systematic and concrete implementation for every steps. For example, how to tune the parameters and how redundancy will affect the quality rating, etc.

Acknowledgments

We thank Prof. Hongbing Xu, Lizhen Xu for discussions and valuable suggestions.

References

1. D.Aebi, L.Perrochon. Towards improving data quality. Proc of the international conference on information systems and management of data,1993,273-281
2. R.Y.Wang. a product perspective on total data quality management. Communications of the ACM, 1998
3. Monica Scannapieco, Antonino Virgillito, Carlo Marchetetti, Massimo Mecella, Roberto Baldoni. The DaQuinCIS architecture: a platform for exchange and improving data quality in cooperative information systems. Information systems 29(2004) 551-582, 2004
4. A.Parssian, S.Sarkar, V.S.Jacob. Assessing information quality for the composite relational operation joins. Proc of seventh international conference on information quality, 2002
5. A.Motro and I.Rakov. Estimating the quality of data in relational databases. In Proceedings of the 1996 Conference on Information Quality, Cambridge, Massachusetts, October 1996, pp. 94-106
6. C.Cappiello, C.Francalanci and B.Pernici. data quality assessment from the user's perspective. Proceeding of the 2004 conference on information quality, 2004
7. R.Y.Wang, H.B.Kon and S.E.Madnick. Data quality requirements analysis and modeling. Proceedings of the Ninth International Conference on Data Engineering, 1993
8. M.Bouzeghoub and V.Peralta. A framework for analysis of data freshness. Proc of 2004 international information quality conference on information system, 2004
9. K.Orr. data quality and systems theory. Communications of the ACM, 41,2.(February 1998)
10. Y.Wand and R.Y.Wang. anchoring data quality dimensions in ontological foundations. Communications of the ACM.volume 39, no 11,1996

11. R.Y.Wang, V.C.Storey and C.P.Firth. a framework for analysis of data quality research. IEEE transactions on knowledge and data engineering, vol 7 no.4 1995 pp.623-640
12. M.Mecella, M.Scannapieco, A.Virgillito, R.Baldoni, T.Catarci and C.Batini. Managing data quality in cooperative information systems. CoopIS/ DOA/ODBASE,2002,LNCS 2519,486-502
13. T.Dasu and T.Johnson, exploratory data mining and data cleaning. John wiley, 2003
14. A.Motro, P.Anokhin, A.C.Acar. Utility-based Resolution of Data Inconsistencies. IQIS 2004: 35-43
15. P.Bertolazzi and M.Scannapieco. introducing data quality in a cooperative context. in proceedings of the 6th internaional conference on information quality, 2001
16. Zoran Majkic. A general framework for query answering in data quality-based cooperative information systems.IQIS,2004
17. Karen Kukich. Technique for automatically correcting words in text. ACM Computing Surveys , 1992.24(4):377 439
18. L. Palopoli, G. Terracina, and D. Ursino. The system dike: Towards the semiautomatic synthesis of cooperative informatimon systems and data warehouses. In Proceeding of ADBIS-DASFAA, pages 108-117, 2000
19. S.Bergamaschi, S.Castano and M.Vincini. Semantic Integration of Semistructured and Structured Data Sources. SIGMOD record28(1):54-49(1999)
20. T.Dasu, T.Johnson, S.Muthukrishnan and V.Shkapenyuk. Mining database structure; or, how to build a data quality Browser. ACM SIGMOD 2002
21. Evoke, Available from http://www.evokesoft.com
22. Amir Parssian, Sumit Sarkar, Varghese S.Jacob. assessing data quality for information products.1999
23. Donald P.Ballou, InduShobha N.Chengalur-Smith, and Richard Y.Wang. Sample-based quality estimation of query results in relational database environments. IEEE transactions on knowledge and data engineering,May 2006
24. Ricardo Baeza-Yates, Berthier Ribeiro-Neto. Modern information retrieval.Addison Wesley,1999
25. Paolo Missier, Suzanne Embury, Mark Greenwood. Guality views:capturing and exploitingthe user perspective on data quality.VLDB,2006

Data Quality for Decision Support –
The Indian Banking Scenario

Hemalatha Diwakar[1], Alka Vaidya[1]
[1]*National Institute of Bank Management, Kondhwa Khurd,*
NIBM post office, Pune, 411048
diwakar,alka, @nibmindia.org

Abstract. To face the challenges posed by new techno-savvy market players, the Public Sector Banks (PSB) and the old private banks in India, have introduced Core Banking Solutions (CBS) to replace disparate branch automation systems. CBS provides centralized online banking operational database which can be exploited for building Decision Support System (DSS) in key areas. While promptness of data is ensured, other data quality needs are to be appraised before implementing any such DSS. Hence an assessment of data quality in two key areas – Customer Relationship Management and Borrower Behaviour was carried out for a sample bank for data profiling, inter-field consistency, attribute value dependent constraints, domain constraints. The study has identified critical areas for data quality improvement both for legacy data that has been migrated and new data being captured by the CBS. Measures for data cleaning and implementation of additional constraints at the database or application level are proposed for improvement of data quality for implementing these DSS.

Keywords: Data quality, Decision support systems, Core Banking solutions, Data constraints

1   Introduction

The onset of technology based Banking solutions, the initiation of financial deregulation, globalization and hence the emergence of new techno-savvy market players in the Indian banking arena, brought in sea changes in the PSBs and old private banks hereafter referred as Indian banks. These banks (with the PSBs alone catering to 72% of the Indian banking business) realized that to achieve maximum business benefits and customer satisfaction, it is prerequisite for banks to have an instant access to the entire bank's transaction level data which in turn can be used for decision support and adept business processes. As a first step, most of them have implemented Core Banking Solutions (CBS) that replaced the disparate Branch automation systems used in branches.

As the next logical step, these banks are planning to use the centralized banking database for prompt and accurate decision support. With 'promptness' being taken care of by the very nature of the centralized online system, the 'accuracy' of the decisions arrived at using the Decision Support System (DSS) will very much depend on the quality of the underlying data. In other words, the success or failure of such DSS projects solely depend on the quality of the data used [1]. Consequently it has become highly imperative to scrutinize the quality of data [2] and understand how effective the decision support system will be in case these data are used as such, before the banks plunge into building such costly Decision Support Systems [3]. The adequacy of data quality and the areas where data quality improvements need to be addressed for two key areas viz., customer relationship management and loan behaviour analysis have been covered in this paper based on a study of sample data from select Indian bank. The work presented here is of unique nature and is vital for the Indian banking industry due to the following reasons:

- The Indian banks are extremely naïve to data quality analysis.

- The size, number and spread of the branches along with the heterogeneity in practices adopted by the bank employees in representing and hence capturing the data in their computerized systems has made the data quality issues all the more distinctive.

- The business practices and business rules used in Indian banking and the data related issues are quite different from the banks in developed countries and hence has to be thoroughly understood before using any data quality related packages, as they are from European and other developed countries. Thus the vendors of such products are as naïve in this exercise as the concerned banks are.

- Also a single product available in the market for data quality may not be adequate for data quality analysis and subsequent corrections [4].

- The practices followed for data capture and representation are almost same for all the Indian banks and hence a study of a sample bank will suffice to prove the point.

The paper is organized in the following way. In section 2, background and current status is presented. The problem definition of two vital business areas related to customer and loans with the necessary decision support requirements are discussed in section 3. The required Meta data and hence the data to be analyzed for the proposed problems are described in section 4 along with the results of the data quality analysis carried out on the sample CBS data of an Indian Bank. The problem kinds emerged out of the data quality analysis is presented along with suitable solutions. The paper concludes with the findings of the study.

2   Background and Current Status

The PSBs are twenty in number in which the government of India is a major stake holder. They are more than fifty years old with some of them as old as hundred. Each of these PSBs has more than thousands of branches spread across the country with the State Bank of India (SBI) and its associates alone having fifteen thousand branches. The old private banks also in the same mold as far as size, reachability and eon are concerned. These Indian banks typically have a three or in some cases four tier organizational structure with a set of branches reporting to a Regional Office (RO) and all regional offices reporting to Head Office (HO). In four tier organization structure, a set of regional offices report to a circle office and circle offices in turn report to the Head office. The Indian Banks do all kind of banking business and are not specialized banks (in just one product) as in the developed countries. Their traditional focus is deposits (liability) and loans (assets).

These banks automated their branches in the early nineties using either Total Branch Automation software or partially automated software systems known as TBA and PBAs respectively for carrying out the branch based banking operations. The TBA package has all the banking operational modules using an integrated branch database at the backend. The maximum business yielding (core) branches were put on TBA, the remaining on PBA with still a few manual branches. All these banks implemented disparate TBA packages at their branches, with some of them having as many as nine different TBAs, with the difference being in the underlying operating system on which they run such as DOS or Windows/Novell/Unix based, and the database being used is either RDBMS or COBOL B-Trieve files. The banks were not networked and hence all of them had islands of information available at branches. The effort to get the consolidated data for reports preparation was so tedious that it used to take more than a couple of months for the bank to know of its entire business status. With the advent of quality network services in the beginning of the new century, the banks started networking their core branches, ROs and HOs and started implementing Core Banking solutions (CBS) recently, a few years back. This has allowed all the banking transactions to take place at a centralized location and thus an instant access to the entire banks' transaction level data for decision support has become easy. Recently, the banks have migrated their current branch level data from their legacy systems (TBA) onto the CBS database for CBS implementation. As there is no overlap on the data among the branches and also no duplication of data (there is no unique customer ID across the bank as India does not have the concept of unique social security number like other developed countries), the data in the CBS are devoid of problems related to data overlapping and duplication that come under "duplicate removal" or "merge-purge" [5].

A study conducted on the TBA to CBS migration with respect to data [6], brought into limelight the following issues:

- Meta data matching of TBA schemas against the CBS database Schema were fully taken care of, as they were crucial for the migration.

- Generally the TBAs, used by the banks took care of unique key constraints, syntactic type checking for attributes and referential integrity [7], and the relation schema in third normal form. But constraints such as domain constraints, any other functional constraints were implemented only through the application programs. As a bank used more than one TBA, the constraints, their implementations were always found to be non homogeneous.

- In order to make the migration smooth, the CBS systems (have ORACLE like DBMS for database management), have defined only the key, referential integrity and foreign key constraints through schema definitions. The other constraints which the bank felt are needed, were incorporated through the application programs. This paved the way for easy bulk loading of TBA data onto the CBS. It also emerged that the data thus loaded from various TBA packages do not comply with all the constraints incorporated in the CBS.

- There are some constraints that CBS packages provide that are found to be not present in the TBAs – for example, the opening of new customer savings account or loan account, deposits etc., have addition constraints. This has brought in incompatibility of the old data migrated from the legacy system against the new data created through CBS data entry applications.

Our survey also indicated that none of the banks did data quality review, let alone data cleaning before they went in for migration. After migrating to

Centralized Banking system, all these banks are planning for Decision Support System (DSS) using CBS data. To start with, data pertaining to only two fields viz., "customer Name" and "Address" are getting cleaned. Hence it has become all the more imperative to

- Demonstrate to the banks that data cleansing on just these two fields are not enough for decision support
- Identify the areas in which the banks want to use the CBS data for decision making purpose; accordingly recognize the relevant data fields, and hence select the underlying data.
- Perform data analysis on these data and show them how good or bad the data are.
- Suggest solutions for rectifying the problem areas.

This exactly being the theme of the paper, two problem domains identified for carrying out this exercise are presented in the next section.

3   Problem Definition

Customer Data Quality Analysis

Customers are the heart of banking business and a decision support system that can assist in introducing right products to appropriate customers, cross selling, expanding customer base, identifying product preferences to customers based on age, geography, occupation etc is a key requirement for the banks.

Loan Behaviour Loans are assets to the banks. Hence it is crucial for banks to study the Borrowers' behaviour to evolve profitable but risk averse loan policies. A DSS with loans data can help the banks

- to identify the profitable sectors in which the bank can give more loans
- to perform segmentation based on loan type to promote or to demote particular loan type.
- provide early warning signals for loans given in a particular sector becoming Non Performing Assets.
- to analyze the behavioural pattern of individual borrowers, their loan preferences.

The relevant data fields that are required for the above mentioned study were identified and hence the relevant data are studied for data quality.

4   Data Quality Analysis of CBS Data for Decision Support

The data fields that are vital in building a customer related DSS, selected from the CBS database schema are two relations Customer and transaction, and are presented in table 1 and 2. Loan master is a relation needed for Loan behaviour analysis is given in table 3.

Table 1. Customer

Sr. No	Field Name	Description
1	Cust_ID	Customer ID
2	Account_No	Account No
3	Br_Code	Branch Code
4	Ac_ty	Type of account such as SB104 for savings account, TLDEP - Term Loan against deposits,
5	Type	Resident Indian, NRI, Staff, ex-staff
6	Ac_op_dt	Account Opening Date
7	Mode	Mode of operation (Single/Joint/Either or survivor, etc.)
8	Nom	Nomination (Yes/No)
9	Address	
10	Gender	Gender
11	Birth_Date	Date of Birth
12	Occupation	Occupation
13	Minor	Y/N
14	City	City of Residence
15	Status	Active/inactive
16	Spouse Name	
17	Number_of_ children	
18	Phone_Number	
19	Salary_range	
20	Pan_card_No	

Table 2. Transaction

Field Name	Description
trans_id	Transaction ID
Opening_Balance	Opening Balance
Narration	Narration
Dr_Cr	Debit/Credit
Amount	Transaction Amount
Ac_Type	Account type
Ac_No	Account No
Trans_Date	Transaction Date

Table 3. Loan Master

Field Name	Description
Type	The type of loan such as Cash Credit, Term Loan, Working Capital, etc.
Ac_type	Further classification of type such as TLDEPO (Term Loan against deposits), Term Loan against government security, SHSG (staff loan for housing), etc.
Account_NO	Account Number
Prin_amt	Principal Amount of loan
Sector_code	Sector code such as agriculture, large scale industry, etc
Subsector_code	Sub Sector code for further classification
Borrower_Catg	Borrower category such as Individual, firm, company, joint, etc.
Last_disb_date	Last Disbursement Date of a loan
No_inst	Number of installments
Start_date	Start date of repayment
Frequency	Frequency of repayment of loan
Inst_amt	Installment Amount
Int_rate	Rate of Interest of loan

4.1   Customer Data Quality Analysis

Common Observations:

Through survey and interviews conducted with the IT department and the branch level employees of most of the Indian Banks, the following observations about the savings bank account holders have emerged [6]:

- As more than 80% of the total customers of these banks are old customers, only the first 9 fields were filled in their TBA systems, (all the remaining fields left blank) and are migrated as such into the CBS. The fields 15 to 20 are filled only after Know Your Customer norms were introduced by the regulators and hence filled only for new customers created (in the last five years or so).

- The address field was filled as string but not in a structured   form (hence needs parsing/data scrubbing to structure it). Also they were not current.

- The city names were not standardized and hence it is very common to find the same city name represented in different ways such as E.g., Bombay, Mumbai, Navi Mumbai, New Bombay, and N.Mumbai etc., all of them referring to Bombay.

- There is no unique customer ID and if a customer has more than one account in the same branch of the bank it is not possible to know all his accounts instantaneously as there is no social security number concept in India. It is very common to find a customer giving his name in different ways in different accounts (savings bank account, deposit account, loan account) that he is holding, in the same branch of a bank (This fact emerged after randomly checking the customer data of a few branches of these banks). The only possible way to rectify it is either to check directly with the customer or use the address (most of the time the address need not be correct or complete or current!) for linking all these accounts.

- In the case of minor (only) the date of birth field was always found filled.

- The Occupation field was having value 'Other" for most of the customers (lack of extensive occupation classification or users "don't care" attitude)

It was evident from these observations that the current savings bank account holding customers' data can not be segmented on age, city; also cross selling, suitable product introduction to apt customers may not be possible due to unavailable/ outdated data.

To do further data quality analysis for the two problems mentioned earlier, actual CBS data of an Indian bank was taken in the same format as given in tables 1, 2 and 3. The data are from two old (more than twenty years), urban, highly profitable branches of the bank located in two different cities. The total customers are 7067 holding 12340 accounts, as of Dec 2006. The number of loans in the Loan master is 3340, with Earliest Loans sanction date: 12-Feb-1997, and Earliest Start date of repayment: 7-Sep-2001. The transaction relation has 369690 records (last two years). The bank had only one major TBA package before it went for CBS and hence the constraints satisfied by the two branches were same.

First a simple data profiling was carried out on the data from transaction and customer relations. Later four key themes related to semantic data quality analysis was described.

Data Profiling

- The date of birth filed was filled only for 2.32% of the customers out of which 1.12% turned out to be minors.

- Occupation field for 82.76%of the customers was found to be filled but 66% of them had value 'Others'.

These results clearly indicate that any analysis based on customer's age and occupation made for decision support is not worthy to pursue. The bank has to follow the customers to get these data filled as it is unavailable elsewhere.

Domain Integrity Constraints

With almost all the domain constraints being preserved by the customer relation, the city field was found out to be an exception. With the data type defined as character, the field was filled by number, name or acronym in the tuples. This was due to constraint on city with all the city names as the possible values. The bank has been using distinct codes for the cities in India and the users typed either code or the name. For example, with 112 for New Delhi as the code, there could be tuples that had 112, or New Delhi or Delhi or N.D as the city value. It is a long process to change them as tools such as [4] can be used.

Attribute Value Dependent Constraints

The functional dependencies are defined among the attributes and they are independent of the individual values that these attributes take in the tuples of any relation. However there are special constraints where the value of an attribute in a tuple determines the value of another attribute in the same tuple. In the banking scenario, such constraints are very common and are to be included for perceiving the real world correctly. They do not violate any functional dependencies and can coexist [8]. A formal definition of the attribute value dependent constraint is given as follows:

If A and B are two attributes of a relation r, then a value dependent constraint between A and B exists

> if for every tuple t $\in$ r, if t.A ="a" then t.B= "b". Or B can also take a value from a selected set of values of the underlying domain of B; or can take the value 'not applicable'.

It is to be noted that there can be a number of attribute value dependent constraints between A and B.

For example two such constraints are

1. 'if Minor is "y" then Mode is any of the three values (Minor and Guardian, Minor and legal guardian, Minor alone or guardian)" and

2. 'If Minor is "Y" then Type is "5".

However the query select count(*) FROM customer where type $\Leftrightarrow$ 5 and minor = 'Y' returned 0.7% occurrences of tuples with contradictory information where field 'Minor' stores 'Y' but 'Type' does not have value 5 in those tuples.

Similarly when the records with any of the three different values of 'Mode' that are reserved exclusively for minor customers were checked for their Minor status, the result showed them as not minors, which is incorrect.

Such incorrect data can be rectified by running appropriate SQL queries to reflect the required changes. For CBS systems, it can be incorporated by allowing default values for Mode to pop up, as soon as the user selects Minor option.

Absence of Auto-Triggering Procedures

Certain attribute values such as minor becoming major, occur with the time. Such changes should be handled by trigger procedures that are to be fired on a daily basis or with the occurrence of an event. However, from the sample data, it appeared that such changes are getting manually carried out by the bank staff with no consistent periodical update policy. Out of the total minors present in the data, 11% should have been shown as 'major' as seen from their birth dates. Again the data can be corrected by running suitable SQL query to reset the value.

Inconsistent Status and Hence Incorrect Value

As a banking rule, the account status of savings bank account holders have to be changed to 'Inactive' value if there is no transaction carried out by the customer for a stipulated time (generally six months or one year). The following query showed that for 11 % records the account status was not changed to 'Inactive' though there were no transactions for those accounts in the last 7 months (base reference is the date the data was received for analysis) in the transaction relation.

> Select count (*) from customer   a
> where a.ac_ty like 'SB%' and a.status = 'ACTIVE' and not exists (select *
> from transaction b where b.ac_no = a.account_no)

Similarly for 0.5% records the 'Inactive' status was not changed to 'Active' even after the customer has carried out a transaction.

An appropriate SQL query can be run on the system to change the status correctly.

From the above mentioned cases, it is clearly evident that these banks can not go ahead for a DSS for customer relationship management purpose without improving the quality of their current data in the CBS. The banks have to define constraints related to the fields in the customer relation, check for correctness, violations if any and rectify them; verify the data in address, telephone and occupation fields for currency, standardize the values for fields wherever needed, collect other data values for fields such as date of birth, profession, family etc., to achieve a meaningful DSS.

4.2 Loan Behaviour Analysis

Frequency Counts

As Borrower category is an important field to determine who are taking loan and what the distribution among these categories is, frequency count for this field in loan relation was carried out. With 73% of tuples having null value in this field clearly indicated the unfeasibility of further analysis.

Table 4: Percentage Distribution of Borrower Category

Borrower Category	%
Null	73.35%
Individual	24.55%
Firms	1.20%
Joint	0.90%

Finding Minimum/Maximum

To check for the presence of any outliers in the numeric and date fields, the minimum, maximum values were calculated. Some of the exceptions that were observed are listed below:

1. Loan amount was found to be zero in 0.6% records. For these records, the start date of repayment was found out to be a future date and hence there were no corresponding transactions in the transaction relation.

2. Rate of interest was found out to be zero in 3.6% records with 1.1% pertaining to staff loans. This excludes those schemes in which staff is offered 0% rate of interest in certain cases (ac_type 'SIFLOAN' offers 0% rate). In case of staff loans, either the data entry operator has entered the account type incorrectly or the rate entered is wrong. However, as a bank rule, the interest rate under any circumstances cannot be zero for on-going term loans.

3. In addition to this, when maximum values were checked for interest rate, 0.3% records in 'TLPER' (Term Loan Personal) account type were found to have greater than or equal to 20% rate of interest. Thus, it was observed that in the same account type the rate varied from 0% to 20%, which is incorrect.

The rectification for all these incorrect values can not be made instantly on the database as bank level loan policy documents, concerned party's loan paper documents along with the presence of authorized bank level personnel are mandatory to carry it out.

Incorrect Data-Business Rule Violations

Start Date of loan was found to be much later than the last date of disbursement in 9% cases, having more than five years difference. These exceptions are permitted only for big industrial term loans or education loans, with moratorium period. However, none of these categories were present in the above said 9%. Such incorrect data will lead to erroneous cash-flow statements required for ALM exercise as Asset-Liability Management (ALM) mainly uses the loan master data. This situation can be taken care of by inducting and checking a vital business rule on the existing records of the loan master.

Attribute Value Based Constraint Violations

In order to do classification of loans as per various sectors, loan schemes, etc. the necessary fields were identified. The important fields and their descriptions are as given below:

Type: This represents loan type, such as, CC, Term Loan, Working Capital, etc. This is the highest level of classification.

AC_type: Further classification of 'Type' is done in this field. E.g. for term loans, it could take values such as TLDEP (term loan against deposits), TLOTH (other term loans).

Sector code: To which sector the loan is given, such as Agriculture, Road and Transport, Staff, Education, Housing Finance, Personal, etc.

Sub Sector Code: Further classification of sectors is done in this code.

To begin with, an attempt was made to classify the loans as per their types which is the top-most level classification. However, from the following table, it can be seen that around 73% records had NULL in loan types.

Further, the values in Loan Types were cross-checked with Account Types. It was found out that the values in two columns are not consistent with each other. E.g. Out of 2.1% Advance against government securities, only 62.5% records showed AC_Type 'TLGOVT' (Term Loan against govt. security). Others included values such as 'Term Loan Others', 'Term Loans against NSC', etc.

Conversely, the records with ac_type 'TLGOVT' did not necessarily have loan type 'Advance against government securities'. They included other loan types such as 'Term Loans', 'Adv against LIC' etc. which is incorrect.

Table 5: Distribution of Loan Types

Loan Type	%
Null	73.65%
Term Loans	18.86%
Adv against deposits	4.49%
Adv against govt. security	2.10%
Adv against LIC	0.60%
Others	0.30%

This clearly shows the absence of suitable value dependent constraints enforcement at the design level. For example, one such constraint could be "if type = 'Advance against Govt. Securities' then ac_type = 'TLGOVT'. Thus in the current data scenario, a query like 'How much is the loan amount against government securities?' will never give the correct amount.

Overlapping of Field Values in Sector-Based Classification

It was found out that, almost 45% records have sector code value 'Others'. This clearly indicates that only 55% records can be used for sector wise classification of loans and these were analyzed further. To begin with, all possible combinations were found out by grouping the three fields Ac_type, Sector code and subsector_code. Some discrepancies that were found are explained with the following example.

ac_type	*sector_code*	*Subsector_code*
TLEDU	Personal	Education Loan
TLOTH	Education	Others

The above two combinations that were present in the CBS database clearly show the ambiguity in defining education loans. In the first case it is evident that education loan is defined through the usage of the fields viz., ac_type and 'subsector_code', whereas in the second case only through Sector_code. The third possibility of all the fields being involved can also be not ruled out. Hence the current data clearly shows that any analysis related to education loan holders in the system will lead to ambiguity. Similar kind of confusing entries were also observed in cases related to staff loans.

This clearly indicates the lack of standardization in data fields' values, absence of constraints indicating their permitted occurrence combinations, need for transformation of certain business rules into appropriate database constraints.

Applicability of Conditional Functional Dependencies

The Indian banks follow different loan interest rates for their employees (staff) and the other customers. However, the interest rate entries for both customers and the staff were found to be the same in all the loan kinds but the loan installment amounts were found to be different. For example if the interest rate is 10%, in case of staff loan, the system asks for the discount that is applicable to the staff and calculates the installment amount and stores the result. Our analysis found out the discrepancy in the installment amounts stored and the above said explanations lead to the need for using conditional functional dependencies to be used for implementing data cleaning in such cases [9]. Similar approach is to be applied to corporate loans as their interest rates are decided based on their credit ratings.

5   Conclusion

In this paper, the data quality analysis carried out on the sample data of an Indian Bank is presented. While the customer related data quality was discussed for all the banks in general, a sample data study indicated the presence of specific shortcomings. The second problem area related to loans was discussed in detail with the presentation of the various data quality analysis results. Wherever possible, suggestions are made for data corrections. A new set of constraints named as attribute value dependent constraints that are very much vital in the banking domain are presented with suitable examples. The findings of both the problems are summarized in the form of a table as given in table 6.

The results very clearly indicate that the banks have to seriously work towards data quality issues before successfully implementing DSS that can bring business benefits. Some of the measures the banks should take in order to improve the quality of data are:

- Check for overlapping of values being present in related fields and resolve the ambiguities – to be done for all data.

- Identify the constraints that are crucial for correctness and consistency of data values – they could be domain level constraints, attribute dependent constraints (such as functional dependencies, that were not used in design but are crucial), value dependent attribute constraints

- Use data profiling tool to collect statistics about the fields that are vital for DSS

- Perform data cleansing; check for their correctness, identify violations if any – specifically to be done for migrated data

- Work out policies for resolving issues related to data ambiguity, inconsistency, incorrect, and not current data.

- Devise mechanisms for collecting data that that are incomplete

- Standardize the values wherever needed.

- Do IS audit, integrity ensuring compliance before and after performing the above said exercises [10], [11], [12], [13].

Table 6. Summary of Findings – Data Quality in DSS

Decision support reports required	Percentage of error free records available	Comments
Customer segmentation based on city/occupation/age	No data available, more than 80% Of records are incomplete	Not possible
Single customer ID linked to all his /her accounts	No	New product induction or cross selling is not possible
Customer city wise segmentation	Address data available	Needs scrubbing, standardization of city names. Currency and correctness are doubtful.
Borrower category wise segmentation	Only in 26% records	Not possible
Sector wise, analysis for NPA identification, also whether loans can be given	55%	Not possible
Loan type wise classification	31% records	Not possible
Individual account wise repayment analysis	All are available	Possible
Reverse analysis of finding out what kind of customers are paying back loan installment in time	Not possible ,	as data about customer not available
Credit amount size wise analysis	Only .6% data wrong	Analysis possible

Last but not the least the bank should check whether the improved data is good enough to accomplish a good DSS or perform a strength and weakness analysis to find out what can be achieved and what can not be, and to what extent and accordingly redefine the targets. If the banks follow these exercises rigorously, they will definitely have a meaningful Decision Support system.

Acknowledgements: this work was done by the first author under the State Bank of India's Information technology chair professorship.

References

1. Sadiq S., Zhou X., Orlowska M.: Data Quality – The Key Success Factor for Data Driven Engineering. In Frontiers of Data Driven Engineering at IFIP International Conference on Network and Parallel Computing, China (2007).

2. Rahm E., Hong H.: Data Cleaning: Problems and Current Approaches, IEEE Bulletin of the Technical Committee on Data Engineering, Vol 23 No. 4, (2000)

3. Benedikt M., Bohannon P., Bruns G.: Data Cleaning for Decision Support. First International VLDB Workshop on Clean Databases, Korea (2006).

4. Raman V., Hellerstein J.: Potter's Wheel: An Interactive Data Cleaning System. Proceedings of the 27th VLDB Conference, Rome (2001)

5. Bohannon P., Fan W., Flaster M., Rastogi R.: A Cost-Based Model and Effective Heuristic for Repairing Constraints by Value Modification. ACM SIGMOD, Baltimore, USA(2005

6. Diwakar H.: TBA to CBS : problems and solutions related to data migration in Indian Banks, Working paper, NIBM, (2007)

7. Date C.J.: Referential Integrity, Proceedings of Seventh International Conference of VLDB, France (1981).

8. Diwakar H: Intentional model – A new database modeling approach ,PhD thesis, Indian Institute of Technology, Delhi(1987)

9. Bohannon P., Fan W., Geerts F., Jia X., Kementsietsidls A.: Conditional Functional Dependencies for Data Cleaning, IEEE (2007)

10. Angeles P., MacKinnon L.: Quality Measurement and Assessment Models Including Data Provenance to Grade Data Sources. International Conference on Computer Science and Information Systems, Greece (2005).

11. Kahn B.K., Strong D.M., Wang R.Y.: Information Quality Benchmarks: Product and Service Performance. Communications of the ACM, Vol 45 (2002) 184-192.

12. Missier P., Oliaro A., Raffa S.: Practical Data Quality Certification: Model, Architecture, and Experience. Proceedings of Information Quality in Information Systems in conjunction with SIGMOD, Chicago (2006).

13. Butler Group: Data Quality and Integrity-Ensuring Compliance and Best use for organizational Data Assets (2006).

An Approach to Cadastral Map Quality Evaluation in the Republic of Latvia[*]

Anita Jansone

University of Latvia, Raiņa bulvāris 19,
Rīga, Latvija, LV-1586

An approach to cadastral map quality evaluation is proposed, which is elaborated and implemented by State Land Service of the Republic of Latvia. The approach is based on opinion of Land Service experts about cadastral map quality that depends on its usage points. Quality parameters of cadastral map objects identified by experts and its limit values are used for evaluation. The assessment matrix is used, which allow to define cadastral map quality that depends on its usage purpose. The matrix is used to find out, of what quality a cadastral map should be in order to be used for the chosen purpose. The given approach is flexible, it gives a possibility to change sets of quality parameters and their limit values as well as to use the approach for other type data quality evaluation.

1. Introduction

Scientific literature identifies several aspects of quality: data quality has several components such as accuracy, relevance, timeliness, completeness, trust, accessibility, precision, consistency, etc. [1], [2]. There are currently two main research streams, which address the problem of ensuring a high level of data and information quality. One is a technical, database-oriented approach, while the second is a management and business-oriented approach. Engineering of information system brings both streams together and addresses issues related to the design and modeling of information systems [3]. Geographical data are data describing an object's spatial location and various properties. Conceptually a geographical database (GDB) may be thought of as consisting of two databases (DB) - one being a common attribute DB and the other is a coordinate DB describing the objects' global locations and dimensions. High quality geographical data will include space location and object properties at given times (where-what-when) [4]. The quality may then refer to the quality of the

[*] The research was partly funded by European Social Fund and Latvian Science Council.

value (how precise the value is, how accurate the label is), as well as to the precision of the coordinates. Existing geographic databases often contain errors due to acquisition source (measuring instruments), data-input process, and information processing [5]. Geographic information quality principles and quality evaluation procedures guidelines are described by standards. The ISO 19113 standard [6] contains principles for describing the quality of geographic data (data quality elements such as completeness, logical consistency, thematic accuracy, position accuracy and temporal accuracy), identifying the quality of geographic data, and reporting quality information. The ISO 19114 standard specifies a methodology for evaluating quality such as process for evaluating data quality, data quality evaluation methods, and reporting data quality evaluation information [7].

Data quality is the degree to which data meet the specific needs of a specific customer. Note that one customer may find data to be of high quality (for one use of the data), while another finds the same data to be of low quality (for another use) [8]. What features do experts working with geographical data (data entry, map drawing, supervision of maps, etc.) use to judge the quality of data? The authors are not aware of any published studies in this area to date. This paper presents an approach (based on opinion of experts) to the evaluation of the quality of cadastral map that predict for the differing levels of quality required of various parameters in order to meet various goals.

The theoretical principles of approach were described in a previous paper [9] that describes the steps that need to be taken to preparing a quality assessment matrix. The subjective assessments of experts in geographical data processing are sought to determine the factors which have the most impact upon the quality of geographical data. When these assessments are evaluated, freed from subjective elements and classified, it becomes possible to specify parameters for the evaluation of data quality, their values, and the required levels of quality. The result of this is a matrix for quality assessment which can be used to determine the data quality level that is necessary for specific purposes or, alternatively, the specific goals for which data at a specific level of quality may be used.

This paper describes how this approach is elaborated and implemented by State Land Service of the Republic of Latvia for cadastral map.

2. An approach to data quality evaluation

The discussion of quality must begin with identification of the objects of interest. Every object will have a number of quality parameters (QP1, QP2, etc.) (Figure 1). Each quality parameter QPn has values taken from one or more sets of values (quality parameter value set) QPnVSk (Table 1), where QPnVS1 may contain the best values. QPnVS2 contains the second best values for some particular goal, etc. [9]

The quality of the object is based upon several or all quality parameters. For instance, an object can belong to the highest level of quality if all of the estimated values of the relevant quality parameters belong to the best sets of values. It belongs to the second level of quality if the values of the relevant quality parameters belong to the second best sets of values, etc.

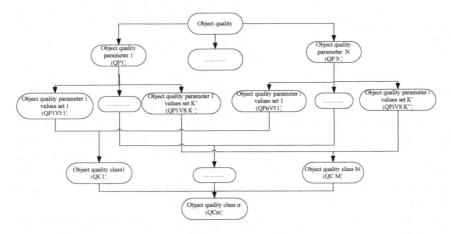

Figure 1. An approach to data quality evaluation

Table 1. Quality parameter value set

Quality parameter (QP)	QPnVS1 (high)	QPnVS2	...	QPnVS K(low)
QPn	from-until	from-until	...	from-until

As a result the object quality evaluation matrix (Table 2) is obtained, which is used to determine, which quality class the object belongs to, as well as to determine, which should be quality parameter values so that the object would correspond to the chosen aim of use.

Table 2. Quality assessment matrix

Object quality class (QC)	QP1	QP2	...	QP N
QC1 (high)	QP1VS1	QP2VS1	...	QP N VS1
QC2	QP1VS2	QP2VS2	...	QP N VS2
...	...	...	...	...
QCm (low)	QP1VS K'	QP2VS K''	...	QP N VS K'''

Quality parameter quality class (QP_QC) depends on a quality parameter value set, to which belongs the quality parameter value:

$$QPn\_QC=1, \text{ if } QPn \in QPnVS1; 2, \text{ if } QPn \in QPnVS2,...., M, \text{ if} \qquad (1)$$
$$QPn \in QPnVSk, n=\{1...N\}, k=\{1...K\}$$

In its turn, object corresponds to the lowest quality parameter quality class:

$$QC=lowest(QP1\_QC, QP2\_QC, ..., QP\ N\_QC) \qquad (2)$$

The aim of object quality evaluation is to determine, which quality class the object belongs to and which aims it can be used for. In order to evaluate an object (Figure 2):

a) check the correspondence of an object to quality criterions, obtain the list or the number of items not corresponding to the quality criterions,

b) evaluate each object quality according to quality parameters and obtain a quality class:

- calculate object quality parameter values, obtain QPn,
- determine, which parameter value set (Table 1) it belongs to, obtain QPnVSk,
- determine, which quality class (Table 2) the value belongs to (1), obtain quality parameter class QPn_QC,
- determine object quality class (2), obtain Object QC.

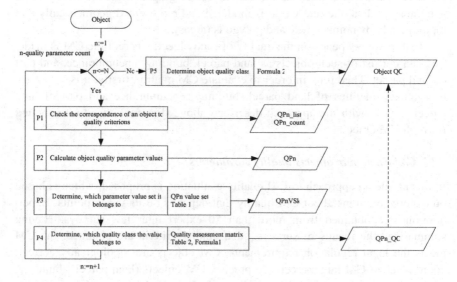

Figure 2. Determine of object quality class

This approach is implemented in State Land Service (SLS) of the Republic of Latvia for cadastral map evaluation and is based on the defined by field experts quality parameters, which describe the usage purpose of a certain cadastral map.

3. Cadastral map quality evaluation in the Republic of Latvia

In the Republic of Latvia, cadastral map (CM) is created in Latvian coordinate system LKS-92 in Transverse Mercator (TM) projection. The following elements are represented in CM: land parcels -boundaries of parcels and their cadastral designations; buildings - outlines of buildings and their cadastral designations; encumbrances - areas occupied by encumbrances of right to use real property and their designations; parts of land parcels- leaseholds and their cadastral designations; boundaries of cadastral territories and cadastral groups. The CM is used to locate cadastral objects with precision so that any changes in boundaries for administrative or other purposes may be accurately described and to describe the relationships between objects for the purposes of environmental and town planning and for various reports. The principles and content of the CM are established by Regulation, which is an ordinance of the SLS of Latvia. The Cadastral IS databases consist of two parts: the textual part (TP) and the graphical part, which includes the CM in vector graphics form [10]. In vector geographical data, the real world is modeled and represented geometrically and topologically by points, lines, and polygons (areas).

CM quality depends on the quality of each object, whereof the CM is made. CM can consist of such objects as land parcel, building, encumbrance, and part of land parcel. Therefore, in order to evaluate CM quality, firstly, it is necessary to evaluate qualities of land parcel, building, encumbrance and part of land parcel – wherewith the approach described above (Figure 1) has to be applied for each CM object.

3.1. *Cadastral map objects quality parameters*

In this article an approach to CM quality evaluation is proposed, which is based on experts' opinions about CM quality that depends on its usage points. Expert opinions are obtained from more than 50 expert interview surveys. Having summarized the results of surveys, such quality criteria are obtained: the CM meets the legal regulation requirements, CM objects are topologically correct, coordinates of CM land parcels are precise, CM objects (land parcels, building, encumbrance and part of land parcel) are in both Cadastral databases and the data is the same – in the TP and in the CM. Quality criteria are given in Table 3.

Table 3. Cadastral map quality criteria

Code	Title
C1	CM meets the legal regulation requirements
C2	CM objects are topologically correct
C3	Coordinates of CM land parcels are precise
C4	Object data in the TP and the CM are identical:
C4.1	A cadastral object (land parcels, building, encumbrance and part of land parcel) has to be in both Cadastral databases – in the TP and in the CM:
C4.1.1	the object marked in a CM has to be in the TP
C4.1.2	the object in a TP has to be marked in the CM
C4.2	Cadastral object data in both Cadastral databases:
C4.2.1	the surveying type for land parcel has to be the same in both databases
C4.2.2	cadastral surveyed land parcels' and parts of land parcels' legal area (indicated in the documents) and area defined by graphical methods (marked in the cadastral map, further in the text – geographical area) cannot be larger or smaller than the acceptable space difference defined in the Regulations
C4.2.3	a building, in both databases, has to be attached to one and the same land parcel

Since the adherence to the Regulations can be checked with the help of available software and topological correctness can also be checked using the latest versions of geographical data processing software, in this article only the quality parameters for the last two criteria (C3, C4) will be considered.

Experts' opinions about CM quality are subjective and therefore have to be structured and, according to normative acts and existing IT solutions in State Land Service, we obtain cadastral object quality parameters (QPn) (Figure 1) – for land parcel (LP) 5 quality parameters are defined (LP_QPn, n=1…5), for building (BD) – 4 quality parameters (BD_QPn, n=1…4), for encumbrance (EB) – 2 quality parameters (EB_QPn, n=1…2), for part of land parcel (PLP)– 3 quality parameters (PLP_QPn, n=1…3) (Table 4).

Table 4. Cadastral map quality parameters

Code	Description	Value excellence – bad	Quality criteria
LP_QP1	Describes how much (%) of CM land parcels are missing in the TP	0%-100%	C4.1.1
LP_QP2	Describes how much (%) of TP land parcels are not marked in the CM	0%-100%	C4.1.2
LP_QP3	Describes how much (%) of CM land parcels surveying type differs from TP surveying type	0%-100%	C4.2.1
LP_QP4	Describes, how much (%) of CM cadastral surveyed land parcels' geographical area is larger or smaller than the acceptable space difference of TP legal area	0%-100%	C4.2.2
LP_QP5	Describes, how much (%) of CM land parcels are cadastral surveyed	100%-0%	C3
BD_QP1	Describes how much (%) of CM buildings are missing in the TP	0%-100%	C4.1.1

Code	Description	Value excellence – bad	Quality criteria
BD_QP2	Describes how much (%) of TP buildings are not marked in the CM	0%-100%	C4.1.2
BD_QP3	Describes how much (%) of CM buildings have different land parcel cadastral designation in TP, to which the building is attached	0%-100%	C4.2.3
BD_QP4	Describes, how much (%) of CM buildings are cadastrally surveyed	100%-0%	C3
EB_QP1	Describes how much (%) of CM encumbrances are missing in the TP	0%-100%	C4.1.1
EB_QP2	Describes how much (%) of TP encumbrances are not marked in the CM	0%-100%	C4.1.2
PLP_QP1	Describes how much (%) of CM parts of land parcels are missing in the TP	0%-100%	C4.1.1
PLP_QP2	Describes how much (%) of TP parts of land parcels are not marked in the CM	0%-100%	C4.1.2
PLP_QP3	Describes, how much (%) of CM cadastral surveyed parts of land parcels' geographical area is larger or smaller than the acceptable space difference of textual part legal area	0%-100%	C4.2.2

LP_QP1, LP_QP2, BD_QP1, BD_QP2, EB_QP1, EB_QP2, PLP_QP1 and PLP_QP2 characterize CM objects completeness [1], [2] in Cadastral IS TP and CM databases.

LP_QP3 and BD_QP3 characterize consistency [1], [2] between TP and CM. LP_QP3 characterize land parcels survey type consistency between in TP and CM. BD_QP3 characterizes building land parcel attachment consistency between TP and CM (in both databases the building has to be attached to one and the same parcel).

LP_QP4 and PLP_QP3 characterize trusted of area (positional accuracy) [5]. LP_QP4 characterize trusted land parcels area. In accordance with the Regulations for CM, the graphical area of a surveyed land parcel listed in the CM (which is calculated on the basis of coordinates) can possibly differ from the legal area of the land parcel shown in the TP (which is declared in legal documents) but within prescribed limits. The admissible level of variation is determined by Regulation. PLP_QP3 characterize trusted part of land parcels area. The purpose of this parameter is the same as that of quality parameter LP_QP4.

LP_QP5 and BD_QP4 characterize accuracy of coordinate (positional accuracy) [5]. LP_QP5 characterize accuracy of land parcels coordinate. The database which includes the graphic component of the Cadastral register includes graphic data to various levels of accuracy. The database of land parcels includes data at three different levels of data accuracy – surveyed land parcels, allocated land parcels, and designed land parcels. The coordinates of the surveyed land parcels are obtained by surveying the relevant parcel with the appropriate instruments. Coordinates of allocated land parcels may have been obtained with older measuring instruments that are no longer in use (field compasses, tape measures), or through conversion from other co-ordinate systems which differ from the specified LKS-92 TM coordinate system. The coordinates of designed land parcels are approximate, because they are usually obtained from ortophoto maps, photo plans or other materials. These coordinates are not based on direct land measurement. BD_QP4 characterize accuracy of building co-ordinate. The database which includes the graphic component of the Cadastral register includes graphic data to various levels of accuracy. The database of building includes data at three different levels of data accuracy – surveyed building, stereo vectorized building, and vektorized building. The coordinates of the surveyed building are obtained by surveying with the appropriate instruments. A stereo vectorized building contour is marked by a stereo tool, but a vectorized building – by scanned material, the building is not surveyed.

3.2. *Cadastral map objects quality parameters values sets*

In collaboration with experts and in the result of experiments, sets of quality parameter values are defined. There are three sets of values for all the parameters: excellent, good, and bad values (Figure 1) QPnVSk, k=1...3.

Parameter values of excellent quality are such as ones, which describe that an object meets quality criteria; values of good quality are such as ones, which do not overrun the defined acceptable error rate, but values of bad quality are such as ones, which overrun the defined rate (Table 5). Parameter value of excellent quality to any quality parameter (except for land parcels and buildings quality parameters of accuracy of coordinate) is 0%, but to the surveyed land parcels and buildings quality parameters of accuracy of coordinate – 100%. Value of good quality to any quality parameter (except for LP_QP5, BD_QP4) is from 0.01% to 5%, but LP_QP5, BD_QP4– from 99.99% to 10%. Value of bad quality to any quality parameter (except for LP_QP5, BD_QP4) is from 5.01% to 100%, but LP_QP5, BD_QP4 – from 9.99% to 0%.

Table 5. Quality parameters values sets

Quality parameters	QPiVS1 excellent	QPiVS2 good	QPiVS3 bad
- LP_QP1, LP_QP2, LP_QP3, LP_QP4, - BD_QP1,BD_QP2,BD_QP3, - EB_QP1, EB_QP2, - PLP_QP1,PLP_QP2, PLP_QP3	0%	0.01-5.00%	5.01-100%
- LP_QP5, - BD_QP4	100%	99.99%-10%	9.99%-0%

Theoretically, object quality parameters and sets of values can be chosen in thousands of variants, but practically, suitable is only such a variant, where parameters are defined by field experts that depends on what object (in this case – a CM) will be used for.

3.3. *Cadastral map objects quality assessment matrix*

Taking into account the purpose of a CM and collaborating with experts, three quality classes of objects are defined (Table 6): high, medium and low (Figure 1) QCm, m=1…3.

Table 6. Quality classes

Quality class		Description
High	1st quality class (QC1)	A CM can be used for making decisions and other activities, where information from the CM is needed
Medium	2nd quality class (QC2)	A CM can be used for making decisions, but it is necessary to be sure about quality of a certain object, which is used for making the decision
Low	3rd quality class (QC3)	A CM cannot be used for making decisions, it can be used to get primary information

Having summarized quality parameter sets of values and quality classes, an object quality assessment matrix (Table 7) is obtained. According to quality parameter values, object quality is: High (QC1), if quality parameter value is excellent – appertains to the set of values QPnVS1. Medium (QC2), if quality parameter value is good – appertains to the set of values QPnVS2. Low (QC3), if quality parameter value is bad – appertains to the set of values QPnVS3.

Table 7. Object quality assessment matrix

Object quality class		Quality parameters value set
High	1st quality class (QC1)	QPnVS1
Medium	2nd quality class (QC2)	QPnVS2
Low	3rd quality class (QC3)	QPnVS3

The main principle of using the quality evaluation matrix – an object corresponds to its quality class, which the worst quality parameter value belongs to.

For example, land parcel quality class 'LP_QC' (Figure 3) depends on the lowest quality parameter quality class (3).

$$LP\_QC= lowest(LP\_QP1\_QC, ..., LP\_QP5\_QC) \qquad (3)$$

Land parcel quality parameter quality class (4) acquire using the sets of values for quality parameters (Table 5) and the quality assessment matrix (Table 7)

$$LP\_QPn\_QC= 1, \text{ if } LP\_QPn \in QPnVS1; 2, \text{ if } LP\_QPn \in QPnVS2; \qquad (4)$$
$$3, \text{ if } LP\_QPn \in QPnVS3, n=\{1..5\}$$

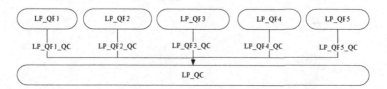

Figure 3. Land parcel quality class

In its turn, quality parameter LP_QPn, n=1...5 is calculated according to define formulas.

Cadastral map quality class (Figure 4.) depends on the lowest cadastral map object quality class (5).

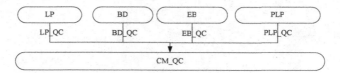

Figure 4. Cadastral map quality class

$$CM\_QC = lowest(LP\_QC, BD\_QC, EB\_QC, PLP\_QC) \qquad (5)$$

Now we can evaluate quality of the chosen CM, because we have defined quality parameters (Table 4) and sets of quality parameter values (Table 5) and object quality assessment matrix (Table 7), and formulas to calculate quality classes.

4. Case study of cadastral map quality assessment

Let's evaluate quality of land parcels in the chosen CM (Figure 5). We have: five quality parameters for land parcels LP_QPn, n=1...5 (Table 4), three sets of values for quality parameters LP_QPn_VSk, n=1...5, k=1...3 (Table 5) and three land parcel quality classes – high, medium, low LP_QCm, m=1...3 (Table 7), CM and TP data, which are given in Table 8.

For demonstrating the approach for CM evaluation let's choose a map, which contains 19 land parcels, 7 buildings, 2 encumbrances and 1 part of land parcel (Figure 5). Data in the CM and TP are shown in Table 8- Table 11.

Figure 5. Detail from the *Durbe* country cadastral map

Evaluation of a land parcel consists of the following steps: 1st step – acquire the number of land parcels in the chosen CM the number of CM land parcels is 19, CM_LP_count=19. Also in the TP the number of land parcels for the chosen region is 19, TP_LP_count=19. 2nd step - acquire how many land parcels do not comply with the proposed criterions, the result is 'LP_QPn_count' or 'LP_QPn_list', n=1...5. Then calculate LP_QPn, how many percents it is and using the sets of values for quality parameters (Table 5) and the quality assessment matrix (Table 7), acquire quality parameter quality class LP_QPn_QC, n=1...5. Finally, get LP_QC (Figure 5).

Table 8. Land parcels CM and TP data

	CM				TP		
Nr	Cadastral Nr. of land parcel	Survey type	Graphical land area m2	Nr	Cadastral Nr. of land parcel	Survey type	Legal land area m2
1	64270020045	allocated	73349	1	64270020045	allocated	82000
2	64270020094	allocated	43925	2	64270020094	allocated	51000
3	64270020103	allocated	91950	3	64270020103	allocated	91000
4	64270020104	allocated	65236	4	64270020104	allocated	59000
5	64270020107	allocated	163022	5	64270020107	allocated	158000
6	64270020117	allocated	40520	6	64270020117	allocated	38000
7	64270020119	allocated	12563	7	64270020119	allocated	15000
8	64270020135	allocated	54089	8	64270020135	allocated	64000
9	64270020146	surveyed	192035	9	64270020146	surveyed	192100
10	64270020148	allocated	81174	1	64270020148	allocated	82000
11	64270020151	surveyed	121532	10	64270020151	surveyed	121600
12	64270020189	designed	19453	12	64270020189	designed	18000
13	64270020190	designed	12905	13	64270020190	designed	13000
14	64270020191	designed	4411	14	64270020191	designed	4000
15	64270020194	allocated	49874	15	64270020194	allocated	53000
16	64270020200	surveyed	2114825	16	64270020200	surveyed	2115500
17	64270020251	designed	119254	17	64270020251	designed	119000
18	64270020266	allocated	322332	18	64270020266	allocated	320000
19	64270020317	surveyed	2690	19	64270020317	surveyed	2700

Table 9. Building CM ant TP data

	CM				TP	
Nr	Cadastral number of building	Survey type	Cadastral number of land parcel	Nr	Cadastral number of building	Cadastral Nr. of land parcel
1	64270020119001	Vectorized	64270020119	1	64270020119001	64270020119
2	64270020119002	Vectorized	64270020119	2	64270020119002	64270020119
3	64270020119003	Vectorized	64270020119	3	64270020119003	64270020119
4	64270020119004	Vectorized	64270020119	4	64270020119004	64270020119
5	64270020195001	Vectorized	64270020317	5	64270020195001	64270020317
6	64270020195002	Vectorized	64270020317	6	64270020195002	64270020317
7	64270020195003	Vectorized	64270020317	7	64270020195003	64270020317

Table 10. Encumbrance CM ant TP data

	CM			TP	
Nr	Cadastral Nr. of LP	Encumbrance code	Nr	Cadastral Nr. of LP	Encumbrance code
1	64270020200	050301 001	1	64270020200	050301 001
2	64270020146	050301 003	2	64270020146	050301 003

Table 11. Part of land parcel CM ant TP data

	CM			TP	
Nr	Cadastral Nr. of part of land parcel	Graphical land area m2	Nr	Cadastral number of part of land parcel	Legal land area m2
1	642700202008001	58766	1	642700202008001	55800

For example, LP_QP1_QC acquisition: a) check, how many land parcels are not in the TP (Table 8). After the check let us make sure that all land parcels in the CM are also in the TP, therefore LP_QP1_count=0, b) calculate the rate LP_QP1=LP_QP1_count/CM_LP_count*100=0/19*100=0%. Using the Table 5 we see that LP_QP1 value appertains to the set of values LP_QP1_VS1 and using the Table 7, the value corresponds to the High class LP_QC1, we acquire that LP_QP1_QC=1.

Qualities of the other land parcel quality parameters class are evaluated in a similar way as the quality of LP_QP1_QC. Qualities classes are given in Table 12.

Finally, land parcel quality depends on the lowest quality class in every quality parameter: LP_QC=MAX (LP_QPi_QC), i=1...5 (Figure 3) and it is Medium class LP_QC=2 - CM (taking into account land parcel quality only), it is permitted to use it for making decisions (TABLE 12), by making sure that land units, which were not surveyed, do not influence the decision. However, if CM usage purpose is not connected with it or land parcels are surveyed (do not take into account LP_QP5, therefore it is not a necessary requirement to be surveyed), then quality of the CM is already High class – LP_QC=1.

If CM usage purpose is connected with involvement of all the objects, then it is necessary to evaluate quality of the other objects. Quality of the other objects is evaluated in a similar way as the quality of land parcels. Quality evaluation of all the objects is given in Table 12.

Table 12. CM *Durbe* quality classes

Land parcel	Building	Encumbrance	Part of land parcel
LP_QP1_QC=1	BD_QP1_QC=1	EB_QP1_QC=1	PLP_QP1_QC=1
LP_QP2_QC=1	BD_QP2_QC=1	EB_QP2_QC=1	PLP_QP2_QC=1
LP_QP3_QC=1	BD_QP3_QC=1		PLP_QP3_QC=1
LP_QP4_QC=1	BD_QP4_QC=3		
LP_QP5_QC=2			
LP_QC=2	BD_QC=3	EB_QC=1	PLP_QC=1

for the chosen CM is acquired taking into account the lowest quality class of each object: CM_QC= MAX(LP_QC, BD_QC, EB_QC, PLP_QC).

As a result we obtain that quality class of the given CM (taking into account quality of all the objects) is the Low class – CM_QC=3 and it cannot be used for making decisions, it can be used to get primary information.

The evaluation method is based on object usage purpose and first, if CM usage purpose does not depend on whether a building is surveyed (quality parameter BD_QP4 is not taken into account), then CM quality is of Medium class – CM_QC=2 and it can be used for making decisions, second, if CM usage purpose does not depend on survey of land parcels and buildings (quality parameters LP_QP5 and BD_QP4 are not taken into account), then quality class is High class - CM_QC=1 and the CM and be used for any purpose.

In order to make everyday use of a cadastral map easy and simple, support software (Data Quality Evaluation Software - DQES) is elaborated for calculating values of quality parameters and for quality class determination as well as for obtaining charts to analyses data and to elaborate a plan for improving data quality. DQES data quality evaluation algorithms tested in practice can be used for supplementing in existing IT solution of SLS.

5. Conclusion

The described approach can be applied to any CM. Quality assessments can be obtained not only for CM of small territories but also for big areas, e.g., cities, regions. The example given in this paper is an assessment of a portion of the Latvia country *Durbe* and reveals where the weaknesses of the map may be.

The insights gained from this analysis are varied. For example, lists of land parcels for which data quality is poor and where data quality needs to be improved in order to useful for given purposes. In particular, approximate calculations can be done estimate the time and financial commitment required to bring a CM to a desired quality. For example, to carry out border adjustments in particular territories.

The approach is based on the opinion of Land Service experts about the cadastral map quality that depends on its usage purpose. Therefore, the quality parameters, quality parameters values sets and quality assessment matrix are well understandable by experts and good to use to evaluate the quality of cadastral map as well as the results of evaluation are clear and understandable. As a result, the experts are interested in the data quality improvement.

The cadastral map quality parameters, values sets, quality classes, quality assessment matrix and evaluation process are comparable generally with ISO standards [6], [7]. You can see the coincidence of the quality dimensions such as completeness between two databases, logical consistency of data values in both databases, and positional accuracy of coordinates and areas, and also the process of the data quality evaluation. The result of the comparison proves that the used approach does not contradict the generally accepted theory. Detailed comparisons will be described in the next research papers.

The elaborated method can be used for quality evaluation of any type objects and the main steps of the methods are: firstly, from experiments obtain subjective opinion about object quality descriptive parameters, which value depends on object usage purpose. Secondly, perform structuring of expert subjective opinion and define object quality parameters and their values, according to object binding normative documents and existing IT solutions in company. Thirdly, together with experiments define object quality classes depending on object usage purposes and what quality parameter values create each quality class, consequently, obtain object quality evaluation matrix, which is used to evaluate the use of an object for the chosen purpose.

Continuing research is aimed at identifying more quality parameters and ensuring that extracted quality parameters conform to the initial subjective opinions of experts.

Acknowledgment

The author would like to thank the scientific advisor Prof. J.Borzovs for advice, the SLS experts A.Sideļska, I.Rudzīte, I.Pauliņa and all Regional Offices experts who took part in the interviews for their assistance in giving freely of their time and expertise with CM.

References

1. J. E Olson, Data Quality: The accuracy dimension, pp 294. Morgan Kaufmann Publisher (2003)
2. C. Batini,, M. Scannapieco, Data Quality: Concepts: Methodologies and Techniques, pp 262. Springer (2006)
3. M. J. Eppler, M. Helfert, B. Pernici, Preface. In: 16th Conference on Advanced Information Systems Engineering (CAiSE'04), DIQ'04 Workshop Chairs, pp 3-4. Rīga (2004)
4. NCGIA Core Curriculum in Geographic Information Science, http://www.ncgia.ucsb.edu/giscc/units/u100/u100_f.html
5. R. Deviller, R. Jeansoulin, Fundamentals of spatial data quality, pp 309, ISTE Ltd (2006)
6. International organization for standardization, Geographic information – Quality principles (ISO 19113:2002), pp 36, CEN (2005)
7. International organization for standardization, Geographic information – Quality evaluation procedures (ISO 19114:2003), pp 71, CEN (2005)
8. T. C. Redman, Data Quality: The Field Guide, pp 223, Digital Press (2001)
9. A. Jansone, J. Borzovs, An approach to geographical data quality evaluation. In 7th International Baltic Conference Databases and Information Systems, pp 125 – 131, Vilnius (2006)
10. Cadastral Template a Worldwide Comparison of Cadastral Systems, http://www.geo21.ch/cadastraltemplate/countrydata/lv.htm

SNP Selection for Psychiatric Disease Association Based on Allele Frequency Plots

E.Fuster-Garcia, Juan Miguel García-Gómez and Montserrat Robles

Biomedical Informatics, ITACA, Polytechnic University of Valencia,
Camí de vera s/n, 46020 Valencia, Spain
http://bmg.webs.upv.es

Mónica Gratacos and Rafael de Cid

Center for Genomic Regulation (CRG), PRBB
Plaça Charles Darwin s/n, 08003 Barcelona, Spain.
On behalf of the Genotyping and Psychiatric Genetics Network

Last years the study of the influence of genetic factors in the susceptibility to some common diseases has been obtaining satisfactory results. These results contribute to the prevention of these diseases as well as to design personalized treatments. The present work introduces a technique based on 2D representations of the genetic data that can contribute to find these disease associations. A real case application is presented in which we analyze the relation between the allele pair values of 748 Single Nucleotide Polymorphisms (SNPs) and the susceptibility to seven common psychiatrical disorders.

Keywords: SNP, Allele Frequency Plots.

1. Introduction

Last decades, many studies show that the appearance of some diseases is influenced by both genetic and environmental factors.[1-4] The study of a selection of the genetic information related to patients with diagnosed diseases can give us information of the causes of these disorders, the relation between them or even a sense of the relation between the established disease classes and new ones more related to genetic traits.

This genetic information is usually characterized by a set of pre-selected Single Nucleotide Polymorphisms (SNPs). It means the kind of nucleotides -A, T, C, or G - that are contained in positions where the genome differs between members of a specie.

Normally these studies involve a large number of SNPs, and therefore a large number of discrete variables that can be analyzed using a wide variety of mathematical techniques. These techniques range from the study of classical statistical parameters to the use of pattern recognition techniques based on artificial neural networks[2] or genetic algorithms.[3,4]

In this work, we present such a kind of study for the case of seven common psychological diseases. The objectives purposed on it are to develop a procedure that allows us to obtain the most correlated genetic markers (SNPs) for each disease (to be able to distinguish between illness and control populations) as well as to obtain a graphical representation of the information contained in the database that helps us to find possible genetic relations between the different diseases.

To achieve these objectives in this paper we define and develop the concept of 2-D Allele Frequency Plots (AFP). These plots allow us to analyze the frequency differences of each allele pair for each SNP between the control population and the illness population, obtaining a distance definition with which we can establish discriminant thresholds. At the same time the possibility to simplify a large genetic database in terms of points in a 2D plot representation constitutes an interesting tool for the obtention of genetic relations between diseases in a visual way.

2. Materials and Methods

2.1. *Database*

The database used in this work is the result of the study realized by the *Genotyping and Psychiatric Genetics Network*. In this database is contained selected genetic information of 3424 patients with psychiatrical diseases diagnosed and some controls. This genetic information is composed by the values of the allele pairs for a set of 748 selected SNPs that can be involved in the genetic susceptibility to psychiatric diseases. At the same time information about the age and gender of each patient is provided. In this study 8 classes have been defined by experts to classify the diagnoses of each patients. These classes are: Substances Disorders, Anxiety Disorders (Panic), Anxiety Disorders (Obsessive - Compulsive), Eating Disorders, Schizophrenia and other psychotic disorders, Bipolarity, Depression and Controls.

2.2. *Allele Frequency Plots*

The basic assumption used in this work is that we can obtain the discriminant SNPs for each disease by the comparison of the appearance frequency of the allele pairs in each SNP for the different population classes. The more allele pairs frequencies between illness and control populations for one

SNP differ, the more this genetic marker could be disease discriminant, and therefore the more frequent allele pair values for each class could contribute to distinguish between the two populations. Based on the assumption just described in this work was considered useful to perform a representation of the allele pair frequencies for each SNP and disease classes, because it has implicit a distance definition that can be use to quantify the significance of each SNP for disease discrimination as well as give us a graphical view of the possible relations between diseases.

3. Procedure

3.1. *Encoding and arranging the database*

The database used in this work is presented as a matrix which elements are the values of the nucleotides for each patient and each SNP (3242 patients x 748 SNPs). Each patient has associated 748 values, one for each SNP analyzed. Associated to this matrix there is a vector with the diagnose (classes explained above) of each patient that have 3242 rows. If someone wanted to study all this information at once in order to represent their relevant information in a plot it would be necessary to simplify the information contained on it doing some assumptions. In this case our first assumption consists on a reduction of the number of variables for each SNP, taking into account that only three possible allele pair types are allowed for each SNP. Instead of the tag of the nucleotides, we will encode the values in the database attending to the frequency of each allele pair for each SNP. This means, for each SNP, the more frequent allele pair is codified as 0, the second one as 1, and the last one as -1. Then from 10 possible tags of allele pairs ($AA, AG, AC, AT, CC, CG, CT, GG, GT, TT$) we have reduced it to 3 $(0, 1, -1)$, without reducing the information contained on it. It is important to notice that for the case of non available data the value assigned was 0 as a mean imputation approach. As a result we obtain a matrix of 3424 rows (patients) x 748 columns (SNPs), composed by $1, -1$ and 0's.

Once the database was encoded we needed to arrange it in order to process it. To do so, the information of the database has to be divided into as many sub-matrices as classes of diseases are defined (8 in this case) i.e. each matrix has to contain the information refereed to the patients of one class (or disease).

Once the data has been rearranged, the simplification of the data can be done using simple statistics calculations. For each sub-matrix we obtain the percentage of each number ($1, -1$ or 0) for each SNP, obtaining as

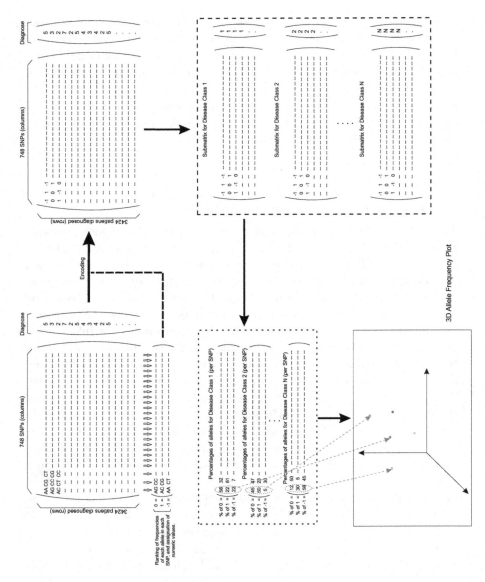

Fig. 1.   Scheme of the encoding procedure.

a result three vectors (one for each number) with the percentage of the corresponding number for each SNP of this classe. See figure 1 for an scheme of the database processing.

3.2. *From 3D to 2D AFP of genetic data*

Defining each axis in a 3D graph as the percentage of 0, 1 and −1, now is possible to plot the data for each SNP and disease as a point in the 3D space.

As can be seen in the figure 2-A all the points are inside a plane. This is because the percentage of 1,−1 and 0's (p_1,p_{-1},p_0) are related by a simple linear equation (see eq 1):

$$p_1 + p_0 + p_{-1} = 1 \tag{1}$$

This means that for each SNP there are only three possible allele pairs, and therefore the sum of the percentages of all of them will be the 100% Note that this is the reason for assigning the most frecuency value to the missing values. If we didn't do it, this relation would not be true and the dimensionality of the problem would increase.

If all the points fall inside a plain it means that there are coordinate transformations that make possible the deletion of one dimension conserving the distances between the points in the space. To do so, we define two vectors in this plane (using 3 points), and calculate their cross product in order to obtain the normal vector to the surface. Then the rotation that reduces the values of two of these normal vector components to zero, is the same that we should apply to our data to pass from 3D to 2D plot. This procedure can be seen graphically in figure 2.

Notice that the variables associated to the axes in the 2D plot are a lineal combination of the variables associated to the axes in the 3D plot and therefore a combination of the percentages of 0, 1 and −1 for this SNP and class. Consequently the position of the points in the AFP plane are refereed to the frequency of the allele pairs for this SNP and disease class and no loss of information is done..

A last step is needed to prepare the 2D AFP to analyze the genetic data presented on it. This step consists in a translation of all the points associated to each SNP so that the point that represents the control population fall in the $(0, 0)$ coordinate. This transform allows us the direct comparison of the points associated to different SNPs in the 2D AFP, and make easier the identification of discriminant SNPs i.e. the further one point is to the $(0, 0)$ coordinate the more useful is their associated SNP to distinguish between the illness population and control ones.

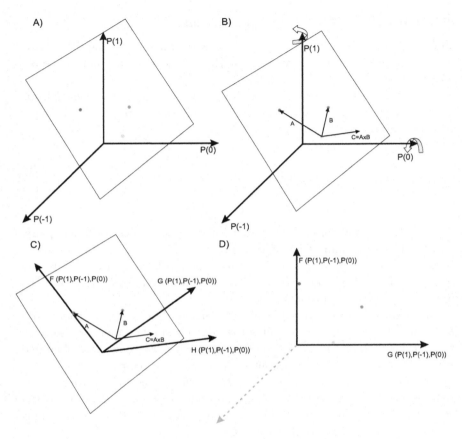

Fig. 2.   Scheme of Rotation Procedure.

3.3. Obtaining information from the AFPs

The AFPs have the advantage to obtain easily conclusions of the SNPs database by only studying the position of the points in the plane. Moreover it is interesting to systematize procedures to obtain relevant information from the plot, in order to enhance the robustness of the conclusions obtained and allow the numerical analysis of the results. To do so we purpose some procedures based in distance definitions and basic geometrical concepts.

3.3.1. *Selection of disease discriminant SNPs and definition of the disease allele pair frequency pattern*

As introduced, the position of the points in the AFP plane are refereed to the frequency of the allele pairs for this SNP and disease class. Then if two points related to the same SNPs but representing the frencuency vectors for different classes are closer, it means that this SNP do not discriminate these two classes. Otherwise, if the two points are distant, it means that exists the possibility to discriminate between the two classes. This behavior of the points over the AFP plane, gives us a visual tool to select disease discriminant SNPs, by only taking into account the distance between points related to different classes. It is important to remember that all points have been translated so the controls ones fall into $(0,0)$ coordinate and therefore the farther the points are to the reference system the more useful these SNPs can be in order to characterize the susceptibility to the disease associated. Now the selection of discriminant SNPs can be done establishing a minimum distance threshold. If the point that represents the Control class for one SNP and the point that represents the Disease class are more distant than the minimum distance threshold then this SNP is candidate for discriminate this disease (see figure 3).

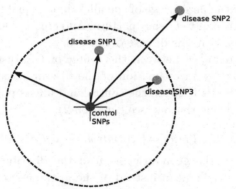

Fig. 3.   Distances between control SNPs points centered in $(0,0)$ and disease SNPs points for a disease class. The further one disease SNP point is to $(0,0)$ the more can it be used to distinguish between control and illness populations. The dashed line is the threshold that will define the borderline between the selected SNPs and the non selected ones.

If this selection procedure is applied to the different SNPs of the database we would obtain a selection of discriminant SNPs for each disease.

The problem now is how to select the threshold value for the minimum distance. If the threshold is too big the set of SNPs candidates for discriminate the disease could not be bigger enough to define the disease susceptibility causes. Otherwise if the threshold is small, then the set of SNPs candidates for discriminate the disease contains a lot of non relevant SNPs that also impede the definition of the disease susceptibility causes.

One way to solve this problem can be to obtain the threshold value that maximizes the discrimination between disease and controls. A procedure that can perform this maximization for each disease can be explained in the following steps:

(1) Obtain a set of selected SNPs by using a particular threshold value: In the 2D AFP this can be seen easily, because the selected SNPs are the ones that fall outside a circumference with radius equal to the threshold value and centered in $(0, 0)$

(2) Obtain the allele pairs for each of these SNPs that represents the disease: In other words, obtain what we define as the *Disease Allele Pattern*, i.e. the pattern of allele pair values that characterize the illness population for the selected SNPs.

(3) Create an histogram for the control patients in which the x axis is represented by the percentage of the allele pairs equal to the defined in the disease allele pair frequency pattern. And create the same histogram for the patients with this disease diagnosed.

(4) Calculate the distance between the center of two distributions: This parameter provides an estimation of the discrimination power of the set of selected SNPs between the control and illness population. Mathematically we define that as (see equation 2):

$$Disc.Power = |(\bar{x}(controls) - \bar{x}(illness))| \qquad (2)$$

where $\bar{x}$ means the geometric mean of the distribution. The reason to use the geometric mean instead of the arithmetic one is because it penalizes the mean value of the distributions far from the normal ones, and therefore avoid the case of only one SNP, where the differences between arithmetic means could be bigger but not significant.

(5) Repeat the same procedure for different threshold values.

(6) Plot the discriminant power value (y axis) obtained for each threshold value (x axis).

(7) Obtain the optimum threshold as the one that maximizes the distance between the two distributions i.e. maximize the discrimination power value.

3.3.2. *Obtaining relations between diseases from the 2D-AFP*

The next question that has to be solved is if there is any relation between the psychiatric diseases analyzed in this study, it means, if some diseases susceptibilities could be influenced by the same SNPs. Only with the comparison between selected SNPs for each of the disease classes results difficult to obtain significant relations about the genetic relations between each of these classes. For example between two diseases that are induced by the same SNPs but with different allele pairs.

In order to find genetic relations between diseases the use of the 2D-AFP could be useful. Only with a visual study of the plot, one can distinguish not only which SNPs are more discriminant for each disease but also if there are some disease classes for which discriminant points fall inside the same region. If this occurs it means that not only the same SNPs are involved in different diseases but also the same allele pairs.

4. Results

4.1. *The 2D AFP*

Following the procedure explained above to re-codify the database in terms of frequencies, to reduce the dimensionality, and to reference the control points to the $(0, 0)$ point of the reference system, we have obtained the 2D AFP of the figure 4 for all SNPs and disease classes.

As it was expected, most of the points fall near the $(0, 0)$ point, i.e. most of SNPs are not useful to discriminate between illness and control populations. Even so, there are a set of SNPs for some diseases that fall far from the coordinate origin and therefore can be discriminant SNPs for this disease.

4.2. *Obtaining the threshold values for each disease*

Once we have obtained the 2D AFP, we have to select the discriminant SNPs for each disease i.e. for each set of colored points we have to define a minimum distance from the coordinate origin (threshold) that split the set in discriminant and not discriminant SNPs for this disease. Using the procedure exposed in the last section we obtain a plot of the discrimination power of the SNPs selected (y - axis) for each threshold value (x - axis). This plot can be seen in figure 5.

On this figure it can be seen that when we increase the threshold deleting the non representative SNPs, the discrimination power increases, but

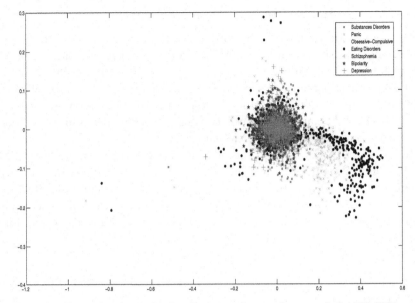

Fig. 4.   2D Allele Frequency Plot for the seven disease classes and the 748 SNPs analyzed in this work. The colors associated to the diseases are: Substances Disorders -red-, Anxiety Disorders (Panic) -green-, Anxiety Disorders (Obsessive - Compulsive) -yellow-, Eating Disorders -black-, Schizophrenia and other psychotic disorders -cyan-, Bipolarity -blue-, Depression -magenta-.

when all the non representative SNPs have been deleted the discrimination power value decreases with the increasing threshold, because we are not considering representative ones .

The values of the threshold distances selected for each disease are resumed in table 1.

Table 1.   Threshold values selected for each disease

	Substances	Panic	Obs-Comp	Eatig	Psychotic	Bipolarity	Depression
Threshold	0.111	0.242	0.244	0.350	0.120	0.086	0.044

4.3. Discrimination between control and illness populations

When we have selected the optimum threshold values for each disease we can see the result of the discrimination between illness and control populations for each disease, showing the histograms in figure 6. These shows the number of patients that have a percentage of coincidence with the Disease Allele Pattern. For this analysis two distribution have been plotted,

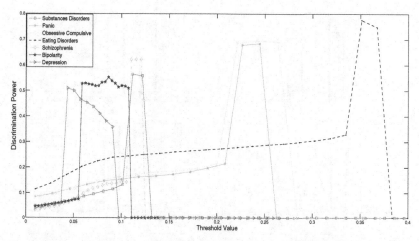

Fig. 5.   Discrimination power of the SNPs selected versus threshold value for each of the disease classes.The colors associated to the diseases are: Substances Disorders -red-, Anxiety Disorders (Panic) -green-, Anxiety Disorders (Obsessive - Compulsive) -yellow-, Eating Disorders -black-, Schizophrenia and other psychotic disorders -cyan-, Bipolarity -blue-, Depression -magenta-.

the first one corresponding to control patients (blue one) and the other one to illness patients (red one). As we mentioned above, if the discrimination is good, the distribution obtained for illness population have to be placed on the right of the histogram (more allele pairs equal to the Disease Allele Pattern) and the distribution obtained for control population have to be placed on the left. This is the case of the Anxiety (figure 6-B), Obsessive-Compulsive (figure 6-C) and Eating disorder (figure 6-D).

4.4. *Relations between diseases*

As was explained above, the 2D AFPs can give information about the relations between diseases. In the particular case of the 2D AFP obtained in this paper (figure 4) some relations can be obtained. After analyzing the AFP, two kinds of points distributions can be dishtingued, the first one is randomly and in most cases near to the coordinate origin and the second one on the right side of the plot formed with points related to Eating disorders, Panic disorders, and Obsessive-Compulsive. The first one does not contain relevant information about relation between diseases because does not exhibit any particular pattern and moreover are not composed by discriminant SNPs. But the second one contains more significant information. If we analyze the points contained in this second region for the three disease

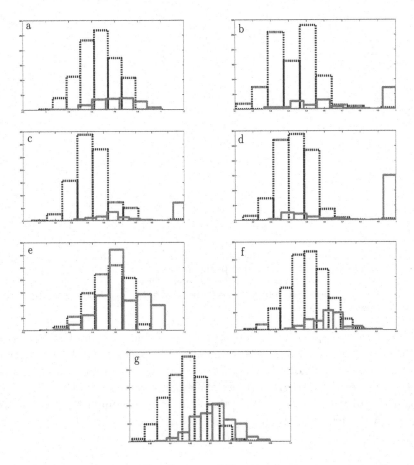

Fig. 6.   Histograms with the distributions of illness and control population for each disease (a.-Substaces, b.-Panic, c.-Obsessive Compulsive, d.-Eating, e.-Psycotic, f.-Bipolarity, g.-Depression). In red (continuous line) the illness sample distribution and in blue (discontinuous line) the control population distribution.

classes represented on it, we find that in most cases the SNPs are common in the three diseases i.e. the genetic susceptibility to these diseases can be generated by nearly mechanisms. Also the fact that all these points fall in a particular region of the 2D AFP means that not only the discriminant SNPs are in most cases common, but also the respective allele pair values that create the disease susceptibility.

5. Conclusions

In this paper a methodology to simplify a large genetic database in terms of points in a 2D plot representation for SNPs disease association studies have been presented. The use of techniques based on these Allele Frequency Plots in the real case of psychiatrical diseases has resulted useful to find discriminant SNPs for the case of Anxiety, Obsessive-Compulsive and Eating disorder (as can be seen in the histograms correspondent to these diseases in figures 6-B, 6-C, 6-D).

Analyzing the point distributions in the 2D AFP also obtains relations between Panic, Obsessive-Compulsive and Eating disorders. This means that the genetic mechanisms that induce the susceptibility in the individious could be similar.

The we can conclude that the 2D AFP technique presented in this paper could constitute a new tool for SNP selection in disease association problems.

Acknowledgments

This research has been partially supported by the Center for Genomic Regulation (CRG).

References

1. The Wellcome Trust Case Control Consortium. Genome-wide association study of 14,000 cases of seven common diseases and 3,000 shared controls. Nature 447, 661-678.
2. Paul R. Lucek and Jurg Ott. Neural Network Analysis of Complex Traits. Genetic Epidemiology 14:1101:1106 (1997)
3. Taane G. Clark, Maria De Iorio, Robert C. Griffi,Martin Farrall. Finding Associations in Dense Genetic Maps: A Genetic Algorithm Approach. Hum Hered 2005; 60:97:108
4. Shital C. Shah, Andrew Kusiak, Data mining and genetic algorithm based gene-SNP selection. Artificial Intelligence in Medicine (2004) 31, 183:196
5. Walter H. Kaye, Cynthia M. Bulik, Lura Thornton, Nicole Barbarich, Kim Masters, Comorbidity of Anxiety Disorders With Anorexia and Bulimia Nervosa. Am J Psychiatry 161:12, December 2004

AUTHOR INDEX